TENNYSON
AT FARRINGFORD

An Exhibition Celebrating the Life of Alfred Lord Tennyson (1809-1892)
on the Bicentenary of his Birth
6 August to 9 September 2009

FARRINGFORD
Freshwater Bay, Isle of Wight

TENNYSON

AT FARRINGFORD

Veronica Franklin Gould   Leonée Ormond

TENNYSON HOUSE

First published on the occasion of the bicentenary of the birth of Alfred Lord Tennyson, 6 August 2009.

Exhibition 'Tennyson at Farringford' 6 August – 9 September 2009.

Catalogue and exhibition written and curated by Veronica Franklin Gould with essay by Professor Leonée Ormond.

Published by:
Tennyson House Publishing
Farringford
Freshwater Bay
Isle of Wight PO40 9PE
tel: 01983 752500
email: publishing@farringford.co.uk

© Tennyson House Publishing 2009.

Text © Veronica Franklin Gould and Leonée Ormond

ISBN 978-0-9563223-0-2

Printed in the UK by:
BAS Fine Art Printers
Unit 2B
Minton Distribution Park
London Road
Amesbury
Wiltshire SP4 7RT

Picture credits:
Balliol College, Oxford 67; Carisbrooke Castle Museum 91; Christie's 59; Dreweatt Neate 22; Hampstead Museum at Burgh House: frontispiece; Haslemere Educational Museum 24; Farringford Estate 33, 43 above, 76; Fine Art Society 57; Gurr Johns, 46 and 47, 85; Julia Margaret Cameron Trust, Dimbola 75; King's College, London, 66; Robin McInnes 71; Philip Mould Ltd. 68; National Portrait Gallery 43 below, 53 below and 93; Graham Ovenden 73; Orchard Brothers 32; Reading Museum Service (Reading Borough Council) 26; Sotheby's 30; Tom Schaefer 11; Trinity College, Cambridge 16 and 96; Watts Gallery 15, 25 below, 51, 56, 63, 64 above and below, 78 below; Andrew Weekes for Lincoln, The Collection and Tennyson Research Centre 8, 17, 20, 28-29, 54, 60, 62, 78 above, 86, 87, 92.

CONTENTS

DIRECTORS' PREFACE

The idea for this our first exhibition came about through our wish to celebrate the bicentenary of Alfred, Lord Tennyson's birth. Farringford was his home for forty years. Here he wrote some of his best loved poems, raised his family, played host to the great and the powerful, and roamed the downs with his dogs and friends. Using this as our reference point we approached Veronica Franklin Gould to be our first guest curator. Drawing on her formidable skills and expertise Veronica has brought together from many sources an exhibition that truly reflects Tennyson's years at Farringford, while giving insight into the many important visitors he attracted. Tennyson's own manuscripts and items of furniture are returning to Farringford for this exhibition. We are therefore exceedingly grateful to the Tennyson Research Centre, Lincoln and Carisbrooke Castle for making this possible.

The winter of 2008 and spring 2009 saw the completion of our first phase of restoration of the house. To coincide with the exhibition opening we decided to restore the library, which houses the exhibition, as closely as possible to Tennyson's day, while sensitively incorporating modern museum standards. The restoration and exhibition are in honour of Alfred, Lord Tennyson's bicentenary birthday.

We wish to thank Ros Tennyson for giving to Farringford Carlo Pellegrini's caricature of Tennyson and for being so supportive of our plans, to thank Elizabeth Hutchings and Dr Brian Hinton for their guidance, friendship and encouragement from our first days on the Island, and to thank all those, without whose generosity this exhibition would not have been possible: Professor Rob Dickens who graciously agreed to lend his beautiful Bowman portrait of Lord Tennyson by George Frederic Watts. Rarely seen, this portrait forms the foundation stone of this exhibition; Grace Timmins of the Tennyson Research Centre, and Dawn Heywood of The Collection at Lincoln for their mammoth support in arranging and lending the poet's letters, manuscripts, family paintings, photographs and furniture and to Dr Mike Bishop, Curator of Carisbrooke Castle Museum for organizing the loan of Tennyson's library furniture, Marion Shaw, Professor Emerita of English at Loughborough University and Chair of the Tennyson Executive Committee for advice and support, to Leonée Ormond, Professor Emerita of Victorian studies at Kings College, London, for her guiding hand, encouragement and generosity in supplying the essay to this catalogue, to Graham Appel of Emerald Construction, to Robin Smith of R.S. Design and Build, to our architect, Richard Nightingale of Cullam and Nightingale, to the Isle of Wight historian Rob Martin, to the crime and prevention officer Michala Bailey and to Corina Westwood, Paul Simpson and John Fletcher at the Isle of Wight Heritage Service for helping us achieve museum display conditions. Finally, we wish to thank André Bourcier and all our staff at Farringford for helping us with the preparations for this exhibition, while at the same time ensuring the smooth running of the hotel.

MARTIN BEISLY AND REBECCA FITZGERALD

CURATOR'S PREFACE

The directors' magnificent restoration of the fabric and decoration of Farringford, bringing fine Victorian furniture, Tennysonian paintings and photographs to the home of the poet laureate Alfred, Lord Tennyson, is the inspiration behind this exhibition, which celebrates his life and work. Thanks to the heroic efforts of Martin Beisly and Rebecca FitzGerald to conserve the library and achieve environmental conditions suitable for exhibition display, we are thrilled to be able to bring here Tennyson's own library furniture and papers.

Special thanks are due to Professor Leonée Ormond, and to Mark Bills, the curator of Watts Gallery for his keen support, offering the choice of the gallery collection, to Dr Brian Hinton, the curator and his team at Dimbola, the Julia Margaret Cameron Museum, for their readiness to advise and lend to the exhibition. For facilitating museum and college loans, we are grateful to Matthew Williams, senior curator of Reading Museum, to Julia Tanner, curator of Haslemere Educational Museum, to Susan Buhr and the Board of Trustees of Hampstead Museum at Burgh House, to Dr Penelope Bulloch, fellow and librarian of Balliol College, Oxford, to Julie Thomas, executive officer at King's College, London and to Vic Harrison, the leading authority on Borzois.

We are grateful in many ways to Iain Cameron, Colin Ford, Christopher Garibaldi, Philippe Garner, Henrietta Garnett, Lady Kennet, Stephen Norman, Graham Ovenden, Rachel Ross, Tom Schaefer, Annabel Watts, to Harry Smith and Louise Davies of Gurr Johns, to Margaret Connell, principal of Queen's College, to Satnam Gill, principal of the Working Men's College and to friends and advisers on the Isle of Wight, to Sir Guy and Lady Acland, Mark Orchard, Dr. Robin Mcinnis, to Elizabeth Hutchings for her generosity, indefatigable research and for drawing our attention to Woolner's original plaster bust of Tennyson.

For excellent catalogue images, we are grateful to Sandy Nairne, Director of the National Portrait Gallery, to Professor David McKitterick, Librarian of Trinity College, Cambridge, to Patrick Bourne and Simon Edsor of the Fine Art Society, and to Lucy Wheeler of Christie's, who has given terrific help at all times. My thanks, too, to Rebecca Fitzgerald and Michael Barker for their editorial eye, and Neville Rolt of BAS Printers. May I add a personal note of thanks to Grace Timmins and Dawn Heywood at Lincoln, for their cheery help with every detail of Tennyson's collection at Lincoln.

VERONICA FRANKLIN GOULD

TENNYSON AT FARRINGFORD

LEONEE ORMOND

In the autumn of 1853, Alfred and Emily Tennyson went house-hunting. Since their marriage in 1850 they had been searching for a home, but, as Emily's journal (cat.1) tells us, all suggestions and recommendations had been followed by disappointments. From March 1851 they lived at Chapel House in Twickenham, where their son, Hallam, was born in August 1852. In October of that year, Tennyson visited Bonchurch in the Isle of Wight. The poet's friend, Richard Monckton Milnes, had published a biography of John Keats in 1848 and it has been suggested that Tennyson's enthusiasm for Keats' poetry had led him to consider settling on the island where Keats had chosen to write. He was told that Farringford House, in the south of the island, near Freshwater, was available for rent from the Seymour family. Tennyson went to look at the house and found a substantial building in the neo-Gothic style fashionable at the turn of the eighteenth and nineteenth centuries. It looked 'rather wretched with wet leaves trampled into the lawn' but he liked it enough to suggest that Emily should travel over and give him her opinion. Freshwater was very remote in the 1850s, and, having missed the steamer from Lymington, the Tennysons made the crossing in a rowing boat. Emily was immediately struck by the view from the drawing room window (cat. 2), and they decided that they would rent Farringford, furnished, with an option to purchase.

Tennyson is a poet of landscape. Views and settings were of great importance to him. Born and brought up in the Lincolnshire wolds, he had found little inspiration in any of the places (Epping Forest, Cheltenham, Mornington Crescent) where he had lived after his family's move south from Lincolnshire in 1837. A compulsive walker, he could now climb daily onto High Down (later given the name Tennyson Down), sometimes pulling Emily with him in a small carriage. Surrounded by trees, Farringford had a sizeable estate, reaching down to the sea. Behind the house was a patch of tangled woodland known as the wilderness through which Tennyson opened up the old paths. Close by, he built himself a summerhouse where he did much of his writing. The Pre-Raphaelite painter, William Holman Hunt,

Fig. 1. (opposite) OSCAR GUSTAVE REJLANDER (1813-1875), *The Tennyson Family Walking in the Garden*, 1863.
Fig. 2. (above) RICHARD DOYLE (1824-1883), *View from Drawing-Room at Farringford*, 1856.

Fig. 3. W. BINSCOMBE GARDNER, Tennyson's dogs outside the summerhouse at Farringford, 1892.

visiting Farringford in 1858, was delighted by the murals which Tennyson had been painting onto the panes of glass: 'writhing monsters of different sizes and shapes, swirling about as in the deep'. The summerhouse no longer survives, but visitors to Farringford tell of dragons, sea-serpents and kingfishers, appropriate subjects for a poet working on a cycle of Arthurian poems, *The Idylls of the King*. In another artistic venture, he made carvings of ivy-leaves in apple-tree wood, and terracotta casts from these were placed round the doors of farm cottages on the estate.

From the start the Tennysons were keen gardeners, with Alfred cutting the grass and rolling the lawns. He would not hear of cutting down the trees which guaranteed his seclusion, even though this would have let through more light for his plants. He was to be seen digging and organising flower and vegetable beds in his gardens. 'I hope no one will pluck my wild irises which I have planted', he wrote, 'if they want flowers there is the kitchen garden – nor break my new laurels etc, whose growth I have watched … I don't quite like children croquetting on that lawn. I have a personal interest in every leaf about it'. Some idea of the garden beds, full of flowers, can be seen in the paintings of Helen Allingham (fig. 4 and cat. 9), who illustrated *The Homes and Haunts of Tennyson* in 1905, after the poet's death.

Tennyson's garden was, as he put it himself, 'careless ordered'. This was an old-fashioned plan rather than the formal style coming into fashion in the 1850s. The natural scheme, with its apparently random shrubs and perennial plants was more like the gardens of today than the set and almost mathematical flower beds of the High Victorian period. At Farringford, as we can tell from Helen Allingham's paintings, flowers were to be found in profusion in the herbaceous borders of the walled garden.

Tennyson's poetry and Emily's journal tell us of their delight in the plants, birds, animals and insects around them. Friends and family related a number of passages from Tennyson's poems to particular aspects of Farringford life. Among them are the references to the cedar tree (cat. 7) and to the white-flowered yucca plant in 'To Ulysses', a poem addressed to a friend, Gifford Palgrave. Tennyson writes of seeing

my cedar green, and there
My giant ilex keeping leaf
    When frost is keen and days are brief –
Or marvel how in English air

My yucca, which no winter quells
    Although the months have scarce begun,
    Has pushed toward our faintest sun
A spike of half-accomplished bells.

In 'The Flower' Tennyson writes of the love in idleness, or heartsease, grown from a seed which he had planted himself. It becomes a symbol for ideas (or his own poetry) which people at first dislike and then steal, copy and devalue.

Once in a golden hour
    I cast to earth a seed.
Up there came a flower,
    The people said, a weed.

To and fro they went
    Through my garden-bower,
And muttering discontent
    Cursed me and my flower.

The flowering yew trees, with the pollen blowing around them like smoke, found their way into two of Tennyson's poems. His son, Hallam, quotes his mother's journal for April 1868: 'There has been a great deal of smoke in the yew-trees this year. One day there was such a cloud that it seemed to be a fire

Fig. 4. HELEN MARY ELIZABETH ALLINGHAM (1848-1926), *Farringford*, c. 1905, watercolour, (Tom Schaefer collection).

in the shrubbery'. Hallam then notes that this was the inspiration for a passage from *The Holy Grail*, part of the Arthurian cycle. The old monk, Ambrosius, tells Sir Percivale that he has lived in the abbey for fifty years:

> 'O brother, I have seen this yew-tree smoke,
> Spring after spring, for half a hundred years'.

The Tennyson memorial in Freshwater Church states that he passed his happiest days at Farringford. One indication of this was his insertion of a new poem in *In Memoriam* (cat. 28). This sequence of poems, making up an elegy for Tennyson's Cambridge friend, Arthur Hallam, was written over many years and finally published in 1850. Its popularity had a part to play in Tennyson's elevation to the position of Poet Laureate in the same year.

In poem II of *In Memoriam*, Tennyson writes of the yew tree, so often found in graveyards, as a symbol of enduring grief. When others trees are flowering in the spring, the yew does not experience a 'glow' or 'a bloom',

> Who changest not in any gale,
> Nor branding summer suns avail
> To touch thy thousand years of gloom.

The experience of Farringford led Tennyson to write a balancing poem which suggests the coming of hope, of relief from the worst effects of sadness. Incorporated into the sequence as number XXXIX, this was written on 1 April 1868 and published in 1869. Tennyson tells us that the yew can also flower, with its 'fruitful cloud and living smoke':

> To thee too comes the golden hour
> When flower is feeling after flower.

Inside the house at Farringford, Tennyson first chose an attic room for his study, but later moved down to the ground floor. A platform was built on the roof (cat. 17) so that he could watch the stars. One of the most remarkable sights he witnessed was the passage of a comet in 1858. For a better view of this, Tennyson climbed up onto the down. On the night of the birth of their second son, 16 March 1854, Tennyson saw Mars in the constellation of the Lion. Lionel had been one of the names considered, and the baby was duly given that name.

Among the poems written at Farringford was *Maud* (cats. 32-33). The extended monologue of a deeply disturbed man, it expresses Tennyson's anger at the Mammonism of the age. The speaker begins with the suicide of his father, who had suffered a financial disaster. He then tells of his love for Maud, the daughter of a neighbour who, he believes, has profited from his own father's fall. There is considerable evidence that the poem refers to a thwarted early relationship between the poet and Rosa Baring, a member of a wealthy family living at Harrington Hall in Lincolnshire. Certain features can, however, be related to the Isle of Wight, including the account of the crashing of the waves onto the shore. Having glimpsed Maud, the speaker stands in his 'own dark garden ground' and hears the sound of the sea:

> Listening now to the tide in its broad-flung shipwrecking roar,
> Now to the scream of a maddened beach dragged down by the wave.

Reviewers complained that these lines were exaggerated, but the scientist John Tyndall confirmed that this effect was not uncommon:

The pebbles and shingles on the beach are mainly flint, and emit a sharp sound on collision with each other. As the billows break and roll up the beach they carry the shingle along with them, and on their retreat they drag it downwards. Here the collisions of the flint pebbles are innumerable. They blend together in a continuous sound which could not be better described than by the line in 'Maud'.

More recently, Richard Hutchings, standing near the site of Tennyson's summer house 'heard the scream of the shingle at Freshwater Bay as it is dragged down by the waves'.

Maud was not much liked by the critics, but the profits from the volume enabled Tennyson to take up his option to buy the Farringford Estate in 1856. Always nervous about money, Tennyson told his brother-in-law: 'We are going to buy this house and little estate here, only I rather shake under the fear of being ruined'. Once they owned Farringford the Tennysons were able to move in their own furniture and to decorate and re-arrange the interior as they wished. One major change came in 1871 when they built a large room for parties and dances with a library above it. The walls of the house slowly filled up with paintings, sculptures and photographs, among them some from the collection of Italian and Flemish old masters amassed by the poet's father.

Maud ends with the speaker joining up to fight in the Crimean War. The Tennysons had heard the sound of cannon practice from across the Solent before the war began, and they learnt of the progress of hostilities from the newspapers. The famous military disaster, the Charge of the Light Brigade, took place on 25 October 1854, and was reported in *The Times* on 3 November. William Howard Russell told the full story there on 13 November and this was followed by other eye-witness accounts. On 5 December, on High Down, Tennyson drafted what has become his best-known work: 'in a few minutes, after reading the description in the *Times*'. The poem was revised over the next two days and then published on 9 December (cat. 0).

Another popular poem written in the summerhouse was 'Enoch Arden' (cat. 38). This is a poem of the sea, telling of a seafarer who tries to set up in business for himself, fails, and so undertakes a voyage on a ship which is wrecked. Enoch spends years on a desert island, is eventually rescued, and comes home to find his wife, Annie, remarried. He does not make himself known to her, and she only learns the truth of his return after his death. We know that the Pre-Raphaelite sculptor, Thomas Woolner, gave Tennyson the story for 'Enoch Arden'. Tennyson himself told a friend that the original events took place in Suffolk. The 'little port' of the poem could be in Tennyson own Lincolnshire, but the landscape of the poem, with its 'Long lines of cliff', its 'chasm', its 'narrow cave' and its beach backed by 'a gray down' is not that of the North Sea coast. It is close to the views that Tennyson's would have seen walking in the area around Farringford. Tennyson would tell friends to 'listen to the sound of the sea' in the line 'The league-long roller thundering on the reef', where he describes the incoming tide on Enoch's island. He was capturing the effect of the waves as they crashed onto the coast of the Isle of Wight.

There were many visitors to Farringford, among them Prince Albert who arrived in 1856, just as the Tennysons were preparing to decorate the house and move in their furniture. Charmed, he left with a bunch of cowslips, promising to bring Queen Victoria over from Osborne (cat.3). Regrettably, this never happened, although the poet made several visits to her. One famous visitor who *did* arrive was Garibaldi, who came in 1864, and planted a Wellingtonia, a hugely tall fir tree, near the house (cat. 58). Tennyson writes of it as

> the waving pine which here
> The warrior of Caprera set,
> A name that earth will not forget
> Till earth has rolled her latest year –

Of the friends who visited Farringford from the mainland many stayed in the house while others established themselves at Plumbley's Hotel in Freshwater. One of the earliest was the painter John

Fig. 5. 'The Meeting of Garibaldi and Tennyson at Farringford', *Illustrated London News*, 23 April 1864.

Everett Millais, who helped the poet to sweep up the leaves and made a drawing of Emily and Hallam Tennyson for Tennyson's 'Dora'. This was among Millais' contributions to Edward Moxon's illustrated edition of Tennyson's *Poems,* published in 1857 (cat . 35).

Two other guests invited to the Tennyson's home were the Reverend Frederick Denison Maurice (cat. 36) and Mary Boyle. Both were sent poems and these tell us what Tennyson most valued about Farringford. Maurice, who was godfather to Tennyson's son, Hallam, was associated with the trends in the Church of England which were described as Broad Church. A liberal, he was one of the founders of the movement for social reform known as Christian Socialism. Shortly before Tennyson wrote the poem of invitation in January1854, Maurice had fallen foul of the Council of King's College, London, for his belief
that damnation need not be eternal. Tennyson drafted and then cut the lines:

> Should half our churchmen bear a spite
> To one so loving of the light
> The bigot needs must bear a spite
> To priests so faithful to the light.

Tennyson sets out to persuade Maurice to leave the 'noise and smoke of town' for Freshwater, where the poet watches the 'twilight falling brown'. Maurice could enjoy the garden and the delights of a civilised dinner table with 'honest talk and wholesome wine' and no 'scandal'. In a poem written much later, in 1889, Tennyson told Mary Boyle to 'change our dark Queen-city' and her 'realm of sound and smoke' for a clear sky, the call of the cuckoo and 'the elm tree's ruddy-hearted blossom-flake . . . fluttering down'.

Local friends were of great importance in providing stimulation for the poet, who was easily bored and often restless. Fossil hunting was a popular pursuit at the time, and the scientist, Dr Robert Mann, and the rector of Brighstone, Mr Fox, were both happy to instruct him. Other friends began to buy or build houses near Farringford. On expeditions to London, Tennyson often stayed at Little Holland House in Kensington, home of Sara and Thoby Prinsep (cat. 54) and a palace of 'high art'. Sara Prinsep was one of the talented and lively Pattle sisters, daughters of James Pattle, an Indian civil servant. The Tennysons knew another of the Pattle sisters, Julia Margaret Cameron, wife of Charles Hay Cameron. The Camerons first rented lodgings in Freshwater in 1857, and then, in 1860, bought two houses and knocked them together to form Dimbola. It was there that Julia Margaret learnt photography, and there are many stories of her pursuit of famous men in the exercise of her art, including, of course, her neighbour and his guests. The Camerons and the Tennysons, parents and children, were constantly visiting each other for more than a decade.

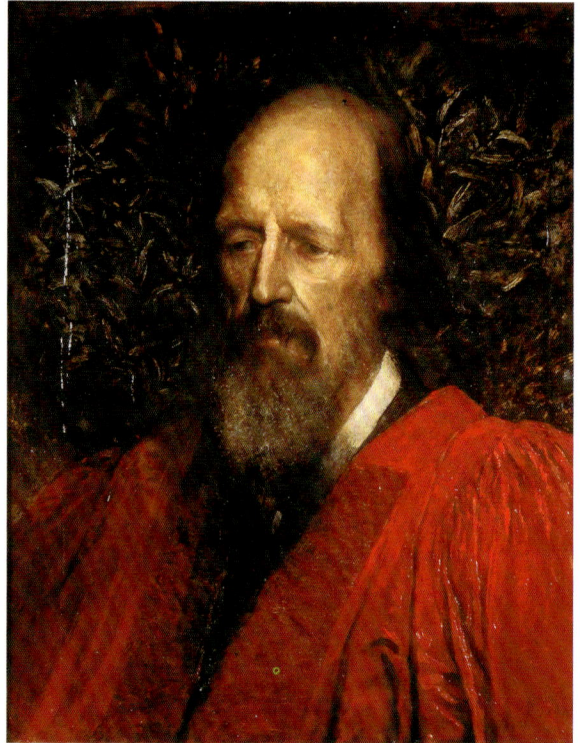

Fig. 7. G. F. Watts, *Alfred, Lord Tennyson*, 1890 (Trinity College, Cambridge).

Through the Prinseps, Tennyson met the artist, George Frederic Watts (cats. 53 and 68), who first painted him in 1858 at Little Holland House, the painter's home for many years. Watts and Tennyson were good friends and, while a guest at Dimbola in 1862, Watts completed a portrait of Emily Tennyson (cat. 51). He then began on another of her husband. Work continued into 1863 on two, almost identical, heads, one, now in the National Portrait Gallery, the other exhibited here from a private collection (cat. 50). These show Tennyson surrounded with laurel leaves, a distant glimpse of the white foam on the beach behind him. In 1864, the artist brought his teenage wife Ellen Terry to Farringford (cat. 69).

When the Prinseps were about to lose their home at Little Holland House, Watts commissioned the architect, Philip Webb, to build a house, The Briary, for them all in Freshwater. Watts and his second wife Mary were at The Briary in 1890 while Watts was painting his last two portraits of Tennyson Mary Watts writes of seeing her husband and his sitter walking towards the Briary. The poet's Russian wolfhound, Karenina (cat. 78), came first and then 'the poet, a note of black in the midst of vivid green, grand in the folds of his ample cloak and his face looming grandly from the shadow of his giant hat' (cat. 76).

The closest of Tennyson's Isle of Wight friends was Sir John Simeon, of Swainston Manor (cat. 67). The two men visited each other regularly, and Tennyson greatly enjoyed Simeon's conversation. More than a year after Simeon died in 1870 he began to write a fine elegy, recalling the day of his friend's funeral. Swainston was famous for its nightingales:

> Nightingales sang in his woods:
> The master was far away:
> Nightingales warbled and sang
> Of a passion that lasts but a day;
> Still in the house in his coffin the
> Prince of courtesy lay.

The poem which Tennyson hoped would close all volumes of his poetry, 'Crossing the Bar' (cat. 41), was written in October 1889 while he was crossing the Solent. He explained to his son the same evening that 'it came in a moment'. Tennyson's gift for natural observation is again apparent, as he tells how the full tide makes no noise and 'seems asleep', almost motionless.

> But such a tide as moving seems asleep,
> Too full for sound and foam,
> When that which drew from out the boundless deep
> Turns again home.

The inspiration for 'Crossing the Bar' came as Tennyson returned to Farringford from his summer home at Aldworth, near Haslemere in Surrey. The increasing popularity of the Isle of Wight had resulted in intolerable incursions upon his personal privacy. A bridge was built so that he could reach the wilderness and the down without encountering his admirers in the lane, but some particularly insistent tourists, anxious to catch a glimpse of the great man, climbed trees or even walked into the garden. From the late 1860s, the family left the island for the summer months, and it was at Aldworth on October 6 1892 that the poet died. A funeral close to Farringford was considered, but the decision was made to bury Tennyson in Westminster Abbey. However, Emily who died four years later, lies in the Freshwater graveyard. On 6 August 1897, a landmark memorial, a tall stone cross was unveiled on Beacon Down as a monument to the poet laureate.

LEONEE ORMOND,
Professor Emerita of Victorian Studies
at King's College, London,
is the author of
Alfred Tennyson: A Literary Life.
.

Fig. 8. F.N. BRODERICK *The Ceremony of the Unveiling of the Monument on Freshwater Down*, 1897.

CHRONOLOGY

1809 Born on 6 August at Somersby, Lincolnshire.

1828-31 Trinity College, Cambridge; member of the Apostles debating society; meets Arthur Hallam; wins the Chancellor's medal for English verse for 'Timbuctoo'.

1827 *Poems by Two Brothers,* with Frederick and Charles Tennyson.

1830 *Poems, Chiefly Lyrical*, first publication by Edward Moxon.

1842 *Poems* establishes Tennyson's reputation as the poet of the age.

1847 *The Princess*, addresses women's education.

1850 Phenomenal success of *In Memoriam* published in May enables Tennyson to marry Emily Sellwood on 13 June; appointed Poet Laureate in November.

1852 Writes 'Ode on the death of Wellington'; Hallam is born in Sussex on 11 May.

1853 Rents Farringford at Freshwater.

1854 Writes 'The Charge of the Light Brigade'; Lionel is born at Farringford on 16 March.

1855 Lear sings; Farringford is redecorated 5-19 February and refurnished April-July; D.C.L., Oxford 18 June; *Maud* published in July.

1856 Woolner begins bust of the poet (completed 1857); Tennysons buy Farringford in April; Prince Albert visits on 13 May.

1857 Begins to translate Aeschylus 'Prometheus Bound' and to write first *Idylls*.

1858 Extra stanzas of 'God Save the Queen', for the wedding of Princess Royal on 25 January; first Watts portrait.

1859 Second Watts portrait; *Idylls of the King* published in July; visitors include Charles Dodgson, Edward Lear, Julia Margaret Cameron, US statesman Charles Sumner, Charles Kingsley, Professor Jowett.

1860 Prince Consort seeks autograph for *Idylls* Camerons move to Freshwater; the Duke and Duchess of Argyll, Lord Dufferin, Henry Taylor, Lear, Lady Charlotte Schreiber visit.

1861 'Ode on the Exhibition'; Prince Albert dies.

1862. 'Dedication' is published with *Idylls*; 'Ode on the Exhibition' soothes the queen; 'Passing of Arthur' for Princess. Interview at Osborne 14 April. Dodgson visits; Watts paints Emily 21-29 November and begins two more portraits of Alfred.

1863. 'Welcome' to Alexandra on her marriage to Prince of Wales; Rejlander photographs Tennyson family in May; Duke and Duchess of Argyll visit; 4 October star-gazing with William Allingham. Translates Homer.

1864 *Enoch Arden* is published; Mayall photographs Alfred, Hallam and Lionel on 14 April, and Alfred in September. Palgrave dedicates *Golden Treasury* to Tennyson; visitors include, Watts and Ellen Terry, Thoby and Sara Prinsep, Professor Jowett, Garibaldi, Henry Taylor, Mrs. Cameron, Allingham, Professor Blackie, Martin Farquhar Tupper.

1865 Watts paints Hallam and Lionel; Tennyson tours Waterloo, Weimar, Dresden; elected F.R.S.

Visitors include Anne Thackeray, Professor Owen, Queen Emma of the Sandwich Islands.

1868 Lays Aldworth foundation stone 23 April. Longfellow, Fraser Tytlers, Prince Alamayu and Captain Speedy visit; unpublished Epigram 'By a Darwinian'.

1869 *The Holy Grail;* Fellow of Trinity; Co-founder of the Metaphysical Society; W. E. H. Lecky.

1870 Sir John Simeon dies 23 May.

1871 Jenny Lind sings.

1872 Tours France and Switzerland; *Gareth and Lynette* published.

1873 Rejects baronetcy offered by Gladstone.

1874 Visits Paris; completes *Idylls;* refuses baronetcy offered by Disraeli.

1875 Writes play *Queen Mary,* a trilogy 'Harold' 'Becket' 'Queen Mary'; tours Pyrenees; W. G. Ward hears reading at Farringford.

1876 *Harold ;* Bateman produces *Queen Mary* at the Lyceum theatre with Irving.

1878 Lionel marries Eleanor Locker.

1879 Boston publisher James T. Fields visits in spring; finishes *The Falcon.*

1880 *Ballads and Poems;* finishes *The Cup.*

1881 Irving and Ellen Terry star in *The Cup* at the Lyceum; Millais portrait; 'Despair' published.

1882 *The Promise of May* at the Globe theatre.

1883 Phillips Brooks visits; September, tours Scotland, Denmark, Sweden in September;

Gladstone offers barony.

1884 *The Falcon; The Cup;* produces *Becket;* 11 March takes his seat at Westminster; votes for extension of the franchise; Hallam marries Audrey Boyle, 25 June; new editions of Tennyson's complete works.

1885 Poem on marriage of Princess Beatrice, *Times* 23 July. 'Vastness'; *Tiresias and other Poems.*

1886 Lionel dies at sea; 20 April; *Locksley Hall, Sixty Years After* and *The Promise of May* .

1887 Summer cruise St David's, Clovelly, Tintagel, Channel Isles.

1888 Suffers from rheumatic gout.

1889 Cruise on Lord Brassey's yacht. *Demeter and other Poems,* includes 'Merlin and the Gleam'. 'Crossing the Bar'.

1890 Tennyson's watercolour sketches are encouraged by Watts; carves brick decoration, moulds of wreath of ivy leaves for Farringford cottage. Watts paints two portraits in May; on 15 May AT records 'The Bugle Song' from *The Princess, The Charge of the Light Brigade, The Charge of the Heavy Brigade, Ask Me No More, Northern Farmer, New Style, Maud, Boadicea* and the *Wellington Ode.*

1891 *Robin Hood.*

1892 *Lines on the Death of the Duke of Clarence.* Tennyson dies at Aldworth, 6 October, buried at Westminster Abbey. *Death of Oenone, Akbar's Dream, and Other Poems.*

1893 Irving and Terry in *Becket* at Lyceum.

1896 Emily, Lady Tennyson dies, 10 August.

1897 *A Memoir* published by his son, Hallam.

FARRINGFORD

Magnetized by the nature around Freshwater on the Isle of Wight, Alfred Tennyson was 44 years old and his wife and secretary Emily, 38, when they moved into Farringford in 1853. Here they raised their sons Hallam and Lionel. For four decades, the poet laureate strode over the downs and, inspired by the sea, rolling downland, cliffs and wildlife, he wrote the poetry of the age. Prince Albert called, the Pre-Raphaelite sculptor Thomas Woolner modelled a fine bust of Tennyson, Edward Lear set his poems to music, John Everett Millais swept the leaves, Professor Benjamin Jowett, the Master of Balliol College, Oxford, came to write, the poet William Allingham transplanted primroses, the unifier of Italy, Giuseppe Garibaldi, planted a tree and Julia Margaret Cameron created remarkable photographs for Tennyson's *Idylls*, and inveigled him to wed the sea.

1. EMILY SARAH, LADY TENNYSON, (1813-1896)
Manuscript Journal, October 1853
ink on paper within cloth-covered boards,
13 ¼ x 8 ⅞ x 2 inches, 33.5 x 22.5 x 5 cm
TENNYSON RESEARCH CENTRE, LINCOLNSHIRE COUNTY COUNCIL (TRC)

Emily Tennyson recalled in her journal and notes for Hallam's *Memoir*, how her husband, searching for a house by the sea, found Farringford, and when he revisited with her, Emily felt compelled to live there. Tennyson agreed to rent the house from the Seymour family in November 1853, and three years later, with the proceeds of *Maud* , took up the option to purchase Farringford, the first home the poet laureate had owned. Notified by friends at Bonchurch, he walked to Freshwater. Alfred found the house looking 'rather wretched with wet leaves trampled into the lawn. However, we thought it worthwhile to go and look at it together. The railway did not go further than Brockenhurst then and the steamer, when there was one from Lymington, felt itself in no way bound to wait for the omnibus which brought as many of the passengers as it could from the train.

> We crossed in a rowing boat. It was a still November evening. One dark heron flew over the Solent backed by a daffodil sky.
>> We went to Lambert's, then Plumbley's Hotel . . . Next day we went to Farringford & looking from the drawing-room window . . . thought 'I must have that view.'

2 JOHN WILLIAM INCHBOLD (1830-1888)
From the Laureate's Home
Watercolour Signed lower left
6 ⅝ x 9 ⅝ inches, 17 cm x 24.5 cm
Farringford Collection, 1869-70

Born in Leeds, Inchbold exhibited at the Royal Academy from 1851. His Pre-Raphaelite landscape *The Moorland, Dewar-stone, Dartmoor* (Tate), painted under the influence of John Ruskin and exhibited in 1854 as *"The Moorland" – Tennyson*, illustrates a scene in 'Locksley Hall'. Inchbold met Tennyson at Tintagel in 1860. Like The Moorland, *From the Laureate's Home* shows how Tennyson's poetry inspired Inchbold. As Alison Smith wrote in *Pre-Raphaelite Vision: Truth to Nature* (Tate, 2004, cat. 130), 'Wordsworth and Tennyson were particularly important with their optic clarity and emotive responses to nature, informing the artist's ability to evoke a mood.' Inchbold, who lived on the Isle of Wight from 1869 to 1870, has captured the atmosphere at Freshwater , the foreground breeze, the calm of the coastline curving towards St. Catherine's Point and, in between, the passion of the sea:

> But such a tide as moving seems asleep,
>   Too full for sound and foam,
> When that which drew from out the boundless deep
>   Turns again home.   'Crossing the Bar'

3. EMILY TENNYSON
Letter to Anne Weld, 15 May 1856.
TRC 686

Negotiations for the purchase of Farringford throughout 1856 were finalized on 3 December. As Alfred and Emily prepared to move out for the Seymours' sale of the contents, the house was in disarray, books unshelved, 'chairs and tables were dancing, sofas stuffed with brown paper, the boys' toys strewn on the floor, when they received a surprise visit from Prince Albert and Colonel Charles Phipps, Keeper of the Queen's Purse.

> Tuesday Prince Albert to call. Two rings at the door and Colonel Phipps announced the Prince who had come to see the [Golden Hill] fort and had heard Ally lived near and had come to ask if he would speak with them. I said I would go and fetch him and asked the Colonel to show Prince Albert into the drawing room and disappeared myself. He was very kind, shook hands with Ally and talked to him very gaily. One of his gentlemen gathered a huge bunch of cowslips which he took into his own hands and said they were so very fine (and so they are) and that they make good tea. We hear this morning he said it was a very pretty place and that he should certainly bring the Queen. It will be a pity if we miss the great honour and pleasure it would be to receive her.

Notified that Her Majesty intended to visit on 17 May, Emily had the children specially dressed and rugs spread between the packages. The stormy weather may have discouraged Her Majesty.

4. EMILY TENNYSON
Letter to Thomas Woolner, 27 May 1856
TRC 2953

The Tennysons engaged the owner of Plumbley's hotel, the finest in Freshwater, to bid on their behalf for much furniture at the Seymours' sale of the contents of Farringford on 26-27 May. Emily confides in Woolner :

> Lambert, the landlord of Plumbley's came here and is bidding for us at the sale at Farringford . . . I think one might soon make the house comfortable again were it not for the ghastly appearance of the drawing room and dining room walls so woefully stained by pictures. Ally has a fancy for the drawing room paper and will not have it changed for he says whatever the paper we had he should not be happy without red and flesh colour and bright frames. Can you recommend him to any pawnbrokers for we must not look to finding our oil pictures in a more reputable quarter.

5. THOMAS WOOLNER RA (1825-92)
Alfred Tennyson, 1856-1857
painted plaster
29 ⅛ x 11 ¾ x 18 ½ inches, 74 x 30 x 47 cm
On loan courtesy of Haslemere Educational Museum: HS.8.2418

Fig. 9. THOMAS WOOLNER, *Medallion of Alfred Tennyson*, 1857.

'Alfred has nobly stood out all the bustle and bother of the removal, helping to unpack and himself to place the things', Emily Tennyson wrote to the sculptor Thomas Woolner on 10 June 1856, after the refurbishment and purchase of Farringford. She goes on to wish him 'good cheer', because after all his struggles, Woolner's bust of the poet laureate, begun on 7 February 1856, marked the turning point in his career. He had trained with Queen Victoria's Sculptor-in-Ordinary William Behnes, and at the Royal Academy Schools and was a founder member of the Pre-Raphaelite Brotherhood in 1848. That year he met Tennyson, Woolner became a lifelong friend, deriving rich intellectual joy from his poetry. Woolner chiefly made a living from portrait medallions, true to nature, capturing the feeling of the sitter, when at last he persuaded Tennyson to sit at Farringford. The sculptor had begun the famous second medallion of the poet, which features as the frontispiece to his *Poems* illustrated by the Pre-Raphaelite colleagues (Edward Moxon, 1857, see cat. 35), when at last, through Emily, Apollo – as Woolner called Tennyson – was persuaded to sit at Farringford for this bust.

Woolner brilliantly captured the poet's frown, and with the curly tangle of his hair and the coat, straining at the button, conveys his natural brooding presence, as though he might stride off the plinth onto the downs, composing 'Merlin and Vivien'. The sculptor had a mould made of the bust in March 1856, and also from the poet's actual forehead and tip of his nose, 'for if I do the bust in marble they will be an assurance to me'. Meanwhile, he reported to Emily in April that this 'striking likeness' was widely admired – Millais 'went quite into raptures' over the bust. Woolner continued to improve it, at Emily's suggestion, thickening the right jaw, and began the magnificent marble bust, (Trinity College, Cambridge) hailed by Ruskin 'a triumph of Art' and displayed at the 1857 'Art Treasures of the United Kingdom' exhibition in Manchester. At the same time, the sculptor made a fine portrait medallion of Emily.

The present plaster, believed to be the original, differs slightly from the unpainted final plaster. (Usher Gallery) Both are inscribed 'ALFRED TENNYSON 1857'. In 1867 Woolner made a replica of the marble bust (Westminster Abbey) and in 1873 carved the bearded bust of Tennyson. (Gallery of New South Wales, Adelaide)

CABINET PORTRAIT

Fig. 10. J.J.E. Mayall, *Thomas Woolner Carving the Bearded Bust of Tennyson*, albumen (Watts Gallery).

6. OSCAR GUSTAVE REJLANDER (1813-1875)
Alfred and Emily Tennyson and their Sons Hallam and Lionel
in the Garden at Farringford, 1863
albumen print
6 ⅜ x 5 ½ inches
16.2 x 13.9 cm
Reading Museum Services
REDMG : 1952.2.1

Alfred and Emily Tennyson much admired the series of photographs Oscar Gustave Rejlander took of their family at the beginning of May 1863. Here they stand outside the house flanked by their sons Hallam, on the right, and Lionel who are wearing their aesthetic, medieval-style tunics and knickerbockers in a similar shade of grey to their mother's dress. These boys are wearing their weekday belts, rather than the crimson sashes and stockings in which they dressed in the evenings and on holiday.

Born in Sweden and trained in Rome, Rejlander settled in Wolverhampton and won fame as a pioneer of high art photography. After Prince Albert accepted his allegory *The Two Ways of* Life (Industry and Dissipation) – a phenomenal composite of sixteen groups and figures – for the International Exhibition of Art Treasures in Manchester in 1857, and sat for a portrait photograph, Rejlander was in demand as a photographer. He set up a London studio.

The photographer took a further group portrait of the family in a glade on the estate, (TRC), as well as individual photographs of the poet in his broad-brimmed hat and cloak, sitting upright in his study chair . He regaled Hallam and Lionel with Norse tales, as he photographed the boys, their golden hair falling over their lace collars and shoulders. Hallam has his father's deep-set eyes and faces the camera, while his younger, tall brother leans dreamily against the pillar of the porch. Rejlander's photographs of the Tennysons were in great demand. 'As these copies are now unattainable I send you this dearest Mrs Tennyson with all my love'.

7. EDWARD LEAR (1812-1888)
Farringford, South Side, 1864
pencil and ink on paper
13 ½ x 18 ¾ inches, 34.3 x 47.7 cm
Signed with monogram, and inscribed 'at 6-7 o/c'/Φαρριγγθορδ/15 October 1864'
and with nature notes
TRC 5786

Edward Lear, the artist famous in his day as the creator of nonsense stories for children, often stayed at Farringford. On 17 October 1864, Lear noted in his diary, 'Perfectly lovely day. Rose shortly after 6 - & at 7 drew in the garden – Hallam & Lionel coming now & then'. His poetic sketch of the south side of the house, which Emily Tennyson also noted in her journal, shows Tennyson's rooftop platform which he built to be able to see the sea to the north and south of the Isle of Wight and at night to study the stars. After his 1861 painting of *The Cedars of Lebanon*, Lear gave magnificent flourish to the Tennyson's cedar and the flowers that grew in profusion around the house and even insect life that fascinated the poet.

Recording the date, the hour and a few notes so that he could add detail and colour later, he instead gave the present sketch to the Tennyson family.

Lear's topographical drawings so impressed Queen Victoria that she had invited him to give her lessons in 1846. His plan to illustrate Tennyson's poetry dates back to 1849; he discussed this with William Holman Hunt, his artistic adviser, in 1852, but it was not until the last decade of his life that Lear embarked on the project. Through the Lushington family – Emily's sister Cecilia was married to the Greek scholar Edmund Lushington – he became a warm friend of the family, composing settings to the poet's verse (cat. 30) and creating a special alphabet for the family. He was delighted when in return for his *Journals of a Landscape Painter in Albania,* the laureate wrote a poem 'To E. L., on his Travels in Greece'.

8. EDWARD LEAR
(1812-1888)
Letter to Alfred Tennyson,
27 June 1864
ink on paper
5 ⅜ x 6 ¾ inches,
13.6x 17.3 cm, folded
TRC 5504

Edward Lear's Nonsense appeal for an autograph contrasts delightfully with the approach of the photographer Julia Margaret Cameron (cat. 66).

9. HELEN MARY ELIZABETH ALLINGHAM, R. W. S. (1848-1926)
The Primrose Path of Dalliance
watercolour
11 ¾ x 10 ¼ inches
30 x 26 cm
Private Collection

Walking out of the breakfast room in his blue cloak with a velvet collar and wideawake hat, Tennyson would cross the oval lawn and pass down this winding path bordered with wild primroses – the family called it 'The Primrose Path of Dalliance' – to the wicket gate . He would then turn left into the bowery lane towards Freshwater Bay, and, as often as not, stop en route at Dimbola, the ivy-clad home of the photographer Julia Margaret Cameron.

William Allingham the poet and diarist recorded visits to the Tennysons from across the Solent at Lymington, where he lived before his marriage to Helen Paterson in 1874. He used to watch the stars with the laureate and help him in the shrubberies, digging up primroses with a knife and spade and transplanting them, wheeling them in a barrow on 3 April 1867, perhaps to this very path. *The Homes of Tennyson painted by Helen Allingham* illustrates twenty watercolours of the Farringford estate and of Aldworth, Tennyson's refuge in the Surrey Hills from the 'Cockneys' who invaded his privacy at Freshwater, and of the poet himself (cat. 42). While Helen Allingham's watercolours of Farringford, painted in the 1880s and 1890s, celebrate the 'golden green' of the trees, and the wild flourish and cultivated beauty, the gay planting – the larkspurs, delphiniums, pinks, eschscholzia - of his kitchen garden beloved by Tennyson, they avoid the storm and passion of his poetry. On the other hand, her husband, who had been a closer friend of Tennyson, liked to challenge the poet and relished his contrasting moods, not least when Julia Cameron brought some firework toys to Farringford. Once alight, they became writhing serpents. She warned that they were poisonous. In defiance, Tennyson put out his hand. 'Don't touch 'em!' shrieked the photographer. 'You shan't, Alfred!' He did. 'Wash your hands then!' The poet rubbed his moustache to antagonize her further.

The present drawing belonged to friends, who used to walk the primrose path with Tennyson. He would stride rapidly, and intrigue them as he stopped to highlight details of geology, insect, bird or plant life along the way.

10. *Tennyson's Wideawake Hat*
felt
6 ¾ x 14 ⅛ inches, 17 x 36 cm
TRC

11. *Tennyson's Cloak*
Wool
54 x 69 inches, 137 x 36 cm
Farringford Estate

12. *Tennyson's Pipes*
clay
5 ¾ and 6 inches, 14.5 and 15 cm
TRC

13. *Tennyson's Spectacles*
wire and glass
1 x 4 ½ x 1/16 inches, 2.5 x 11.5 x 0.15 cm
TRC

14. after THOMAS WOOLNER RA (1825-92)
Alfred Tennyson
Cameo of 1856 medallion
2 ⅜ x 2 inches, 6 x 5 cm
TRC

15. *Tennyson's Quill Pen*
13 ⅜, 34 cm long
TRC

16. *Lord Tennyson's Visiting Card*
Ink on paper
1 ½ x 2 ½ inches,
Inscribed in Emily Tennyson's hand
'Mrs Orchard /with best thanks for the
beautiful roses and old print'
Orchard Brothers

Emily, Lady Tennyson's message to Mrs.
Orchard thanking her for roses epitomises the
poet's life at Freshwater. Orchard Brothers, the
shop, a stone's throw from Farringford,
founded by William Orchard in 1865, supplied
provisions to Farringford. Tennyson brought
the American poet Henry Wadsworth
Longfellow (cat. 72) to buy clay pipes; and
other patrons among Tennyson's circle recalled
today by Orchard Brothers were Sir John
Simeon, G. F. Watts, Ellen Terry, Anny
Thackeray and the prime minister William
Gladstone.

Fig. 11. Orchard Brothers, established 1865.

17. WILLIAM TROST RICHARDS (1833-1905)
Near Tennyson's Home, Isle of Wight, 1880
watercolour
6 ¼ x 7 ⅝ inches,
16 x 19 cm
Farringford Estate.

These mature trees once formed an avenue to an earlier Farringford house. Tennyson loved visiting his old shepherd Paul and hearing him call each sheep and identify its individual character and expression. As the shepherd tended his flock, he would listen to the song of thrushes, yellow-hammers, tits, blackbirds, and cuckoos before dawn; and in the evening she watched rooks whirl and soar high into the sunset.

      The American landscape and marine artist William Trost Richards, born in Philadelphia, exhibited at the Royal Academy from 1860 to 1900. He painted this watercolour at a time when he had a studio in London. Having painted *King Arthur's Castle* , the year before, Richards was clearly interested in Tennysonian themes.

18. MYLES BIRKET FOSTER RA (1825-1899)
Freshwater Bay, Isle of Wight
c 1894
watercolour heightened with bodycolour
7 ¾ x 11 ¾ inches,
Private Collection

Myles Birket Foster made designs to illustrate Tennyson's 'Break, Break, Break' and 'The Reapers' in the 1850s, but the publisher Edward Moxon's plan to have Birket Foster illustrate the entire volume of *Poems* was shelved. The present watercolour was shown in the 1894 exhibition of the Royal Society of Painters in Watercolours.

In the early 1890s Birket Foster joined the poet on his walks at Freshwater. This would have been the view from the cliff, where they began to make their descent to Freshwater Bay, here by no means 'the scream of a maddened beach dragged down by the wave', but 'a light upon the shining sea'. Although Tennyson was now unwell and had to be accompanied by a nurse (cat. 76), the artist recalled that he still set off at a great pace and conducted a spirited discourse. 'Does it ever strike you, as a landscape painter,' observed the laureate, when they were walking in dark woodland towards bright sunshine, 'that going through an avenue of trees into the light beyond is like passing through the grave into Eternity! '

TENNYSON'S LIBRARY

Fig. 12. W. BINSCOMBE GARDNER, The poet's dogs, writing desk and furniture in 1892, now on display in his library at Farringford. (*The English Illustrated Magazine*).

19. EMILY TENNYSON
General Order for the Domestic Staff
ink on paper
7 x 9 inches, 18 x 22.8 cm, folded
TRC: N16A

20. EMILY TENNYSON
Catalogue of Tennyson's Library, 1855
ink on paper
sheet, 12 ¾ x 8 ¾ inches, 32.5 x 22.2 cm
TRC: N19

21. EGB
Catalogue of Books, Drawing room and Library
18 July 1857
ink on paper
sheet, 7 ¼ x 4 ⅜ inches, 18.5 x 11.2 cm
TRC: N20

22. ALFRED TENNYSON
List of Books Wanted [to research *Idylls*]
ink on paper
7 x 4 ⅜ inches, 18 x 11.2 cm
TRC N17

23. ALFRED TENNYSON
Sheet A, Catalogue of My Books, c 1861
ink on paper
sheet, 7 x 4 ⅜ inches, 18 x 11.2 cm
TRC: N25

24. EMILY TENNYSON
'*Books in Ally's Study*, March 1874
ink on paper
6 x 4 ⅜ inches, 15.5 x 10 x 1 cm
TRC: N22

25. AUDREY TENNYSON (1854-1916)
Farringford Library Catalogue, 1887
Ink on paper
9 x 7 ⅛ inches, 23 x 18.2 cm
TRC: N23

26. EMILY TENNYSON
Letter to Hallam Tennyson, 7 March 1871
Ink on paper
7 x 4 ½ inches, 18 x 11.5 cm, folded
TRC: 281

Emily Tennyson writing to her son Hallam at Marlborough College, discusses plans for his father's grand new library at Farringford. They have engaged the architect Alfred Waterhouse and are about to knock down part of the greenhouse (see cat. 7), link the remaining section with an archway leading into a large family room for children's romps, battledore and shuttlecock, as well as theatrical performances and dances. Tennyson's library above would be approached – as it is today – by the main staircase; and for a quick escape from approaching visitors, the poet is to have the private turret staircase on the south side, which leads down to the garden. Overriding Waterhouse's 'vagrant imagination', the Tennysons have decided to revert to their original plan for Papa's room. Emily explains, 'The lower room is to be treated as a hall with the stairs running in it which will make it more spacious for dancing or acting, and when this and the greenhouse are lighted the suite of rooms will be very pretty, I hope.' Her sister's 'rascal' of a builder has estimated the cost of building works at £386, plus a few shillings and pence and works began in March 1871.

27. ANNE ISABELLA THACKERAY, LADY RITCHIE (1837-1919)
Records of Tennyson, Ruskin and Browning, London, Macmillan, 1892
Octavo
Courtesy of Henrietta Garnett

After the death in 1863 of William Makepeace Thackeray, Julia Margaret Cameron, the Tennysons' close friend and neighbour, invited the novelist's daughters Anne 'Anny' and Harriet Marian 'Minnie' to stay at her cottage in Freshwater and welcomed them into the Tennyson circle. Herself a writer, Anny wrote a novella based on their lives at Freshwater, and illuminated the atmosphere at Farringford in *Records of Tennyson, Ruskin and Browning*: 'walked with Tennyson along High Down, treading the turf, listening to his talk, while the gulls came sideways, flashing their white breasts against the edge of the cliffs, and the poet's cloak flapped time to the gusts of the west wind.

> 'The house at Farringford itself seemed like a charmed palace, with green walls without and speaking walls within. There hung Dante with his solemn nose and wreath; Italy gleamed over the doorways; friends' faces lined the passages, [portraits by G. F. Watts and photographs by J. M. Cameron] books filled the shelves, and a glow of crimson was everywhere . . . As we sit around the twilight [drawing-room], with its great oriel-window looking to the garden, across fields of hyacinth and self-sowed daffodils toward the sea, where the waves wash against the rock, we seem carried by a tide not unlike the ocean's sound; it fills the room, it ebbs and flows away; and when we leave, it is with a strange music in our ears, feeling that we have for the first time, perhaps, heard what we may have read a hundred times before.

THE POETRY OF ALFRED, LORD TENNYSON
Published by Edward Moxon & Co., of Dover Street, London.

At Farringford, Tennyson continued to revise his first epic poems *The Princess* (1847) and the seminal *In Memoriam A.H.H.* (1850) for which he was elevated to poet laureate and summoned to comfort Queen Victoria a dozen miles away after the death of the Prince Consort. Here, during the Crimean War, he created the popular 'The Charge of the Light Brigade' and successful, but controversial monodrama *Maud*, which enabled him to purchase Farringford. While Tennyson was reluctant to have his earlier poems illustrated, Millais's sketch of young Hallam at Farringford met with his approval in Moxon's 1857 edition of the *Poems* illustrated by the Pre-Raphaelite artists. Having published 'The Lady of Shalott' in 1832, and a further three Arthurian subjects in the 1842 *Poems*, Tennyson worked on his magnum opus *Idylls of the King* for the rest of his life, while artists – among them Gustave Doré and the poet's friend and neighbour Julia Margaret Cameron – created albums to illustrate it. *Enoch Arden*, written in the summerhouse, was one of some 200 illustrations Edward Lear created from his poems in the last decade of his life. As Tennyson was returning to Farringford in 1889, he composed the poem 'Crossing the Bar', which he instructed Hallam to place at the end of all his works.

Due to myopia, the laureate held his manuscript close to his eyes when reading poems to visitors. James Thomas Fields, his American publisher, recalled in 1859 that Tennyson spoke in 'a low unmelodious thundergrowl, but when he chooses he can melt as well as rasp with his Lincolnshire tongue', that 'his gait moves with his voice' and that he read 'Come into the garden Maud'. in a kind of chant. 'His Knowledge is most wonderful, and when he talks he says things that are apt to send a thrill with the words'.

Opposite: Cat.36B

28. *In Memoriam A. H. H.*, 1850
8vo, bound proofs, trial book
TRC: P216, cat. 4060

In Memoriam A. H. H. – the title suggested by Emily Tennyson – was published to phenomenal acclaim in 1850 and led to Tennyson's elevation as poet laureate. A sequence of poems dedicate to the memory of his Cambridge friend Arthur Henry Hallam, who died in Vienna in 1833, *In Memoriam* was revised after publication at Farringford, and gave great comfort to Queen Victoria after the death of Prince Albert in 1861. *In Memoriam* is both personal and universal. 'It is rather the cry of the whole human race rather than mine', Tennyson explained to James Knowles, his architect and editor of *Nineteenth Century*. Private grief swells out into thought, and hope for the whole world.' Beginning with death, the funeral of Hallam, it ends in promise of a new life, 'a sort of Divine Comedy, cheerful at the close.'

29. *The Princess: A Medley*, 1859
Quarto, 188 pages with 26 illustrations engraved on wood by Daniel Maclise
Farringford Estate

Tennyson revised *The Princess: A Medley* (1847) – the story of a university of women into which no man may set foot – more than any other poem. Challenging traditional values at a time when formal education was the preserve of men, his story appears stridently feminist until the principal, Princess Ida, gives in and marries the prince.

The year after publication, Queen's College was founded by Frederic Denison Maurice, initially to certify governesses. Writing in the format he would later use for *In Memoriam* and *Maud,* Tennyson later added songs and lyrics and the present volume, the seventh edition, is the first with illustrations.

30. 'Tears, Idle Tears', *Poems and Songs by Alfred Tennyson, Set to Music by Edward Lear*
London, Cramer & Co, 1853, 1878 edition, 8 pages
13 ¾ x 9 ¾ inches, 35 x 25 cm
Farringford Estate

'Tears, Idle Tears', from *The Princess,* is one of the poet's finest lyrics, expressing, Tennyson explained, the yearning young people sometimes feel for that which has passed. The first of a series of four set to music by Lear, it is the sheet music in Holman Hunt's *The Awakening Conscience* (Tate, 1853). Lear had audiences weeping. Tennyson liked his settings because 'they seem to throw a diaphanous veil over the words – nothing more'. As Lear was composing music for *Maud* (1858), singing to the notorious Farringford piano, the laureate marched up and down, and joined in. 'Lear, you have revealed more of my Maud to myself!' Lear lamented to Emily, perhaps because she herself was a fine pianist and also composed musical settings to her husband's poems, that 'the P.Laureat [sic] hath only an ancient & polykettlejarring instrument.' Julia Margaret Cameron solved the problem in June 1860 by getting eight men to carry her own piano from her house.

31. *'The Charge of the Light Brigade'*, 1854
second galley proof, annotated by John Forster and another hand
10 ¼ x 5 ¼ inches, 26 x 13.5 cm
TRC: C3868.

'The Charge of the Light Brigade' was Tennyson's most popular poem. Before the birth of his second son Lionel in March 1854, the poet built a shelter of rushes for his wife to enjoy the downs, and the excitement of the nearby cannon practice for the Crimean War. Within months, Tennyson read reports of the battle and terrible defeat at Balaclava. The Light Brigade had misunderstood an order to prevent Russians from removing British guns and instead, on 25 October, attacked the main Russian gun emplacement. *The Times* reported that only 198 of the 670 soldiers returned – in fact 552 of 607 soldiers survived.

Shocked at the thought of the Brigade riding to certain destruction, and that British soldiers should be victims of 'some hideous blunder' – or as he misrecalled in splendid rhythm, 'someone had blundered'– Tennyson composed 'The Charge of the Light Brigade' on 5 December as he paced over the High Down. The next day he learned the true figures. Emily, sending the poem to John Forster for publication in the *Examiner* (6 December), explained that Alfred would like to retain 'six hundred' for the metre, though it could be corrected to 700. The 'six hundred' stayed, but Tennyson regretted having agreed to omit 'Some one had blundered' for his 1855 revision and so reinstated it in 1856.

Into the valley of Death	'Forward, the Light Brigade!
Rode the six hundred	Take the guns,' Nolan said:
For up came an order which	Into the valley of Death
Some one had blundered	Rode the six hundred

'The Charge of the Light Brigade', which Tennyson sent out to comfort the troops, established the 'charge' as a military disaster, the subject of many a heroic painting, as Leonée Ormond observes, yet pointing out its success in dashing the confidence of the Russian cavalry.

Maud, A Monodrama

Maud, published in July 1855, soon after he was awarded a D.C.L. at Oxford, was Tennyson's most experimental poem, in concept and construction, and was his favourite to recite to friends and visitors. Pressed by Sir John Simeon (cat. 67) to weave a story around 'Oh! that 'twere possible', a lyric he had composed in the 1830s –here expressing anguish after Maud's death –Tennyson built up what he called a 'Drama of the Soul', a tale of love thwarted by Mammonism. *Maud* not only addresses humanity, it reflects the poet's despair over the death of his father, his brother's insanity, and the poverty that had kept him from Emily, driving him to despair until the proceeds of *In Memoriam* enabled them to marry. Likening the morbid, poetic protagonist to Hamlet, he explained that he was 'the heir of madness, an egoist with the makings of a cynic, raised to a pure and holy love which elevates his whole nature, passing from the height of triumph to the lowest depth of misery, driven into madness by the loss of her whom he has loved, and, when he has at length passed through the fiery furnace, and has recovered his reason, giving himself up to work for the good of mankind through the unselfishness born of a great passion.'

Emily was spot on in her suggestion to Edward Moxon in August 1855, that *Maud* would not be understood for some time, 'I am prepared for a different tone of criticism from the many, but in the end I shall not wonder at its being popular.' Tennyson did receive distressing criticism, yet *Maud* sold so well he was able to purchase Farringford. There are glimpses of the house and of the Isle of Wight and in the poem, 'the house half hid in the gleaming wood', 'the scream of a maddened beach dragged down by the wave' and 'the daffodil sky'.

32. *Come into the Garden, Maud', 1855*
Facsimile
Trinity College, Cambridge

  Come into the garden, Maud
    For the black bat, night, has flown
  Come into the garden, Maud
    I am here at the gate alone,
  And the woodbine spices are wafted abroad,
  ..... And the musk of the rose is blown.

33. *Maud has a Garden of Roses,* 1867
Thirteenth [Fourteenth] edition, page 49, XIV 1.
Printed proof,
8 ½ x 7 inches, 21.6 x 17.7 cm
TRC: P22, cat.4147

Maud appeared in three parts in 1865. In his search to perfect his poetry, Tennyson valued the final version above the first edition.

34. THOMAS WOOLNER
Letter to Emily Tennyson, 8 October 1855
ink on paper
7 ⅛ x 4 ⅜ inches, 18 x 11 cm, folded
TRC 6101

Woolner, seeking Emily's advice for improvements to his new medallion of Tennyson (Fig. 9), to send to the publisher Edward Moxon as the frontispiece of an illustrated edition of Tennyson's *Poems* (1857, cat. 35), writes 'How vilely "Maud" has been abused: dingy clouds trying to blot out the light of a star. I saw in a letter of Cobden's the other day he had been snarling at the Poet he cannot comprehend . . . The poem has been more delight to me than anything I have known for a long long time . . . Mrs Browning told me she thought it much the finest work he had ever done.' The sculptor thanks Tennyson for sending a copy of *Maud* and wished he made a bust of the poet when at Farringford. It would have taken no longer and been 'a fifty times better work and more important. I shall never have such a fine head again.' (cat. 5).

The Moxon Tennyson

35A. *Poems*, 1857 (open at 'Dora')
Octavo, 375 pages, with illustrations by Thomas
Creswick, John Everett Millais, William Holman
Hunt, William Mulready, John Callcott Horsley,
Dante Gabriel Rossetti, Clarkson Stanfield, and
Daniel Maclise
Farringford Estate

35B. *Poems*, 1857 (Title Page)
inscribed 'To the dear Signor with Xmas
greetings from Julia Margaret Cameron'
Watts Gallery: GFW/6/18

Moxon persuaded Tennyson to let him publish an
illustrated edition of his 1842 *Poems*, which appeared in
spring 1857, with Woolner's medallion as its
frontispiece and illustrations by traditional and Pre-
Raphaelite artists.

John Everett Millais sketched Emily and Hallam
Tennyson at Farringford in November 1854. Hallam
appears as the child 'Dora' in the *Poems*. Millais helped
sweep the leaves, later painting *Autumn Leaves*
(Manchester City Galleries). 'Is there any sensation more
delicious than that awakened by the odour of burning
leaves?' he enthused to Hunt, who also illustrated the
Poems and gave a drawing of Millais at this time (Fig. 13).
Emily, keen to see the illustrations, wrote to Woolner on
27 May 1856, 'I long to hear what you think of them.
Some of Millais' seem to us very fine', though Ruskin
found Tennyson quivering with fury: 'Painters ought to
attend to at least what the writer *said* [–] if they couldn't,
to what he meant'.

Fig. 13. William Holman Hunt (1827-1910)
Sir John Everett Millais, 1853
(National Portrait Gallery)

Idylls of the King

A cycle of twelve narrative poems on the legend of King Arthur, *Idylls of the King*, symbolizing the spiritual development of man, was the seminal work that fascinated visitors to Farringford and established Tennyson as the most famous poet in the land, earning the nicknames 'Alfred the Great' and 'King Alfred'. Although he had published four Arthurian poems before coming to Farringford: 'The Lady of Shalott', 'Sir Launcelot and Queen Guinevere', 'Sir Galahad' and 'Morte d'Arthur', it was there in 1855 that he resolved the shape of the cycle. By 1859, 'Enid', 'Vivien, 'Elaine' and 'Guinevere', proof-corrected in the summerhouse with Emily and published under the title *Idylls of the King*, consolidated his popularity. The French artist Gustave Doré brought out volumes of engravings for each poem. While the laureate was composing the Arthurian poems that had been in his mind since the age of 24, and Julia Margaret Cameron was photographing family, friends and neighbours to illustrate them, visitors felt they were witnessing history in the making.

Nervous about interpreting the quest for the Holy Grail, Tennyson did not tackle the subject until September 1868, pressed by Emily and friends, by which time he regarded *The Holy Grail* – published in 1869 with 'The Coming of Arthur, 'Pelleas and Ettarre' and 'The Passing of Arthur' – as one of his most imaginative poems 'I have expressed there my strong feeling as the Reality of the Unseen. The end, when the king speaks of his work and of his visions, is intended to be the summing up of all in the highest note by the highest of human men. Three lines in Arthur's speech are the (spiritually) central lines of the Idylls:

> In moments when he feels he cannot die,
> And knows himself no vision to himself,
> Nor the High God a vision.'

Rearranging the poems, Tennyson finished up with twelve, plus his 'Dedication' to the memory of Prince Albert, a great fan of the *Idylls*, and a poem 'To the Queen'; and in 1891, a year before his death, he added the last Arthurian line to the epilogue, 'Ideal manhood closed in real man' to clarify the humanity of the king.

GUSTAVE DORE (1833-1883)
Idylls of the King,
Edward Moxon 1867-1869

36A *'Vivien Encloses Merlin in a Tree'*, 1867
engraving for *Vivien*
plate, 9 ½ x 7 ⅛ inches
24 x 18 cm
Farringford Estate

36B *'Geraint and Enid Ride Away'*, 1869 (illustrated on page 38)
engraving for *Enid*
plate, 9 ¼ x 7 inches
23.5 x 17.8 cm
Farringford Estate

Gustave Doré, one of the foremost and prolific illustrators of the day, was born in Strasbourg and worked as an engraver in Paris, illustrating Rabelais, Balzac, Milton's *Paradise Lost* and Dante's *Inferno*. Following commissions to illustrate the works of Lord Byron (1853), Doré and an English Bible (1866), an exhibition of his work at the Egyptian Hall in Piccadilly in London (April 1868) led to the opening of the Doré Gallery at 35 New Bond Street.

Idylls of the King were among Doré's finest inspirations, and he exhibited the drawings at the gallery, though Hallam Tennyson notes in *A Memoir* that his father was not entirely satisfied with his illustrations to the *Idylls*. However, on 7 July 1869 he and his father breakfasted with Doré at the Moulin Rouge in Paris, where they visited the artist's 'enormous studio' in the rue St Dominique and parted with perfect cordiality. 'We were much pleased with the good Doré.'

37A *Alfred Tennyson,* registered 3 May 1865
albumen, 17 ½ x 14 ⅛ inches, 44.5 x 36 cm
Julia Margaret Cameron Trust, Dimbola

37. JULIA MARGARET CAMERON (1815-1879)

Alfred Tennyson's Idylls of the King and Other Poems, London, Henry S King, 1874

'Dedicated by gracious permission to Her Imperial and Royal Highness Victoria The Crown Princess of Germany and Prussia and Princess Royal / Julia Margaret Cameron' Norman Family Collection.

In the summer of 1874 Tennyson suggested to his friend and neighbour Julia Margaret Cameron, a photographer of international standing (see page 73), that she provide illustrations for a twelve-volume cabinet edition of *Idylls of the King*. 'Now *you* know Alfred, that *I* know that it is immortality to me to be bound up with you.' She threw herself into the project, making 245 photographs to achieve twelve successful prints. Freshwater friends, family and even the Yarmouth porter 'King Arthur' were summoned to her lens. Agnes Mangles's sensual expression and pose as the seductress Vivien seems heightened by a sense of foreboding. Might Merlin, Julia's husband eminent Charles, burst into laughter again? Charles Hay Cameron wore a wonderful purple caftan, whether posing or not. He had been the first legal member of the Council of India and was now absorbed in the classics, which Tennyson loved to discuss with him, describing Cameron as 'a philosopher with his hair dipped in moonlight'

Only three thumbnail woodcuts from Mrs Cameron's photographs were used, so on the poet's advice, she had King publish two folio albums of full-size lithographic reproductions from them, the first for Christmas 1874 and the second album in May 1875. The photographer provided handwritten inscriptions 'From Life Registered Photograph Copy right [sic] Julia Margaret Cameron' and titles below, with excerpts from the text opposite. Colin Ford writes in *Julia Margaret Cameron, The Complete Photographs* that her 'pioneering attempt to bring to life the allusive poetry of Arthurian legend through photography . . . provide[s] a convincingly human and contemporary interpretation.'

38. *Enoch Arden, and Other Poems*, 1864
Octavo, 178 pages
Farringford Estate

Based on the folk myth suggested by Woolner in the 1850s, of a sailor who returns to find his wife, believing him drowned, married to another man, *Enoch Arden* embodies Tennysonian preoccupations with anxiety over a father's return from the brink of the grave, or indeed returning to a woman whose happiness he might destroy – his own impoverished state having at first kept him from Emily. *Enoch Arden*, Tennyson's most extended and successful poem, was chiefly written in the summerhouse in Maiden's Croft during the winter of 1861-1862, though Emily made subsequent enquiries about the training for a boatswain. She impressed upon her husband that *Enoch Arden* must be the title poem of his next volume, (which included 'The Brook', 'Aylmer's Field, 'The Northern Farmer Old Style, 'Sea Dreams', The Golden Supper' and 'Boadicea'), rather than 'Idylls of the Hearth'. It was published in August 1864 and before the year was out 60,000 copies were sold. Edward Lear wrote on 26 June 1884, from San Remo where he had named his final home Villa Tennyson, that he was painting a picture sixteen feet by nine, of a scene in Enoch Arden's Island.

39. ROBERT BROWNING (1813-1889)
Letter to Alfred Tennyson, 13 October 1864
ink on paper
7 x 4 ⅜ inches, 18 x 11.2 cm, folded
TRC 6296

Tennyson has sent *Enoch Arden and Other Poems* to the poet Robert Browning, who, wishing an autograph for his son, comments on each poem. He finds "Enoch" perfect, but

> the "Farmer" taking me unawares, astonishes me more in this stage of our acquaintanceship. How such a poem disproves the statement in that strange mistake of yours – the flower – apologise = "steal your seed"? – as if they want flower-seed in a gum-flower manufactory! One might cabbage out a tolerable rose, by adroit scissor-work on starched calico, after studying in your gardens of Gul, - but the seed for the phenomenon itself comes from a place that was

never reached from the top of a wall, you may be sure. "Boadicea", the new metre is admirable – a paladin's achievement in its way = I am thinking of Roland's Pass in the Pyrenees, where he hollowed a rock that had hitherto blocked the road, by one kick of his boot – so have you made our language undergo you.

Do but go on . . . Ever yours, on the various stations of this life's "line", and, I hope, in the final refreshment-room ere we get each his cab and drive gaily off – "Home", where call upon Robert Browning.

40. GEORGE FREDERIC WATTS OM RA (1817-1904)
Letter to Alfred, Lord Tennyson, 25 December 1885
ink on paper
7 x 4 ½ inches, 18 x 11.3 cm
TRC: 6276

Tennyson sent a signed copy of each volume to G. F. Watts, a warm friend since the 1850s, both epitomizing the Victorian era in their art. Like the poet laureate, the Royal Academician sought to express great moral truths, the highest mind of humanity, ferociously attacking evils of the day. (cat. 53). Watts, the subject of unprecedented retrospective exhibitions in London and at the Metropolitan Museum of Art in New York in the 1880s, writes to thank Tennyson for *Tiresias and Other Poems*, with the signature reserved for friends, 'Signor' within an artist's palette.

'in the whole list of English Poets & authors (including foreign as far as I know them) there are none from whose works I derive greater pleasure & Profit with affectionate regards to Lady Tennyson & indeed all Farringford. believe me to be Yours most sincerely G.F. Watts Signor'.

41. *Crossing the Bar*, 1889
ink on paper
6 x 4 inches, 15.2 cm x 10 cm
TRC M11

Thinking about the 'Moaning of the Bar' on his way from the mainland to Farringford in October 1889, the octogenarian poet showed these four timeless verses to his son after dinner. 'Crossing the Bar' had come to him in just a moment. As ever, the surrounding sea is foremost in his mind, the Pilot humanity's ever-present 'Divine and Unseen' guide. 'That is the crown of your life's work,' exclaimed Hallam. Tennyson instructed him to place 'Crossing the Bar' at the end of all editions of his poems. (See page 96).

42. HELEN MARY ELIZABETH ALLINGHAM, R. W. S. (1848-1926)
Lord Tennyson in his Study at Farringford, 1890 (frontispiece)
watercolour
12 ⅜ x 9 inches, 31.4 x 22.8 cm
inscribed 'Sketch from life by Helen Allingham; in his study, Farringford, Isle of Wight'
Hampstead Museum at Burgh House: 19989.65.P

PHOTOGRAPHED FROM LIFE BY W. BAMBRIDGE, AT WINDSOR CASTLE MARCH 28. 1862.

DIEU ET MON DROIT

"May all love,
His love unseen but felt, o'ershadow Thee,
The love of all Thy sons encompass Thee,
The love of all Thy daughters cherish Thee,
The love of all Thy people comfort Thee,
Till God's love set Thee at His side again."

Tennyson.

Published by permission.   Ent.ᵈ at Stationers.

Prince Albert of Saxe-Coburg-Gotha (1819-1861)

Prince Albert, a great admirer of Tennyson's poetry and of the view from the drawing-room at Farringford, had been an early, impromptu caller. Particularly moved by the 1859 *Idylls of the King*, which he used to recite himself, the prince wrote to ask the poet laureate to autograph his copy. Tennyson's 'Dedication' written soon after Albert's death at the request of his second daughter, Princess Alice, helped to soothe the queen, and was published as the opening poem of *Idylls of the King* from 1862 and thereafter.

43. JOHN JABEZ EDWIN MAYALL (1813-1901)
Prince Albert of Saxe-Coburg-Gotha (1819-1861), May 1860
albumen
9 ⅞ x 6 ⅛ inches, 25 x 15.5 cm
Watts Gallery: COMWG2008.163.403

44. PRINCE ALBERT OF SAXE-COBURG-GOTHA (1819-1861)
Letter to Alfred Tennyson, 17 May 1860
7 x 4 ½ inches, 18 x 11.7 cm, folded
TRC: 4695

The Prince Consort, in his letter asking Tennyson to autograph his personal copy of 1859 *Idylls of the King*, indicates the seminal influence the poet laureate's impassioned recreation of the Arthurian legends had on the Victorian people.

> You would thus add a peculiar value to the book containing those beautiful songs, from the perusal of which I derived the greatest enjoyment. They quite rekindle the feelings with which the Legends of King Arthur must have inspired the Chivalry of old, whilst the graceful form in which they are presented blends these feelings with the softer tone of our present age.

45. PRINCESS VICTORIA, PRINCESS ROYAL OF GREAT BRITAIN, CROWN PRINCESS OF GERMANY (1840-1901)
Letter to Alfred Tennyson, 23 February 1862
ink on paper
7 x 4 ¾ inches, 18 x 12 cm, folded
TRC 4796

Queen Victoria's eldest daughter writes after Prince Albert's death that Tennyson's words were 'drops of balm on the broken and loving'. His first Idylls on the ideals of womanhood enchanted her parents. She now sees her father as King Arthur, and cannot forget his recitation of 'Sir Launcelot and Queen Guinevere' - 'hearing those grand and simple words in his voice! To all who possess a quick and deep appreciation of the beautiful it is a pleasure too great and intense'.

46. PRINCE ALBERT OF SAXE-COBURG-GOTHA
The Principal Speeches and Addresses of His Royal Highness the Prince Consort with an Introduction Giving Some Outlines of His Character, London, John Murray, 1862
Presentation copy, inscribed by Queen Victoria, 'To Alfred Tennyson, Esquire / Who so truly appreciated / this greatest, purest and best of men / from / the beloved Prince's / broken-hearted widow / Victoria Rg, / Osborne 9 December 1862'
TRC 400

On 14 January 1863, Emily noted in her journal that the queen's lady-in-waiting Lady August Bruce came to luncheon, bringing 'what is to us beyond price' the queen's gift of the Prince Consort's speeches inscribed with kind words written by HM's own hand [above], also a beautiful photo of herself and three of her children with Ally's lines' under it. (cat. 41). Before this final verse of the 'Dedication', a prayer giving all-embracing comfort to the queen, the penultimate verse is more personal:

> Break not, O woman's heart, but still endure
> Break not, for thou art Royal, but endure,
> Remembering all the beauty of that star
> Which shone so close beside Thee that ye made
> One light together, but has past and leaves
> The Crown a lonely splendour.

47. WILLIAM BAMBRIDGE (1819-1879)
Queen Victoria and her children, Princess Alice, Princess Victoria and Prince Alfred, Mourning the Death of Prince Albert, 28 March 1862 (illustrated on page 47)
albumen
6 ¾ x 5 ⅜ inches, 17 x 13.7 cm
Private Collection, London

Queen Victoria (1819-1901)

'I loved the voice that spoke', Tennyson wrote to Lady August Bruce after his first interview with Queen Victoria at Osborne House on 14 April 1862. The myopic poet continued, 'I yet could dimly perceive so great an expression of sweetness in Her countenance'. The Duke of Argyll, a close associate of Prince Albert and friend of Tennyson, had relayed the queen's command, summoning him to her residence a dozen miles north east of Farringford. 'I am a shy beast and like to keep to my burrow', Tennyson replied to the Duke, who advised him about protocol and recommended that he spoke to the monarch as a bereaved woman, rather than the Queen of England.

Her Majesty recorded in her diary that Tennyson was 'very peculiar looking, tall, dark, with a fine head, long black flowing hair and a beard – oddly dressed,' but quite unaffected. Seeing Prince Albert reflected in his memorial to Hallam 'even to his blue eyes', she told Tennyson of the comfort she derived from *In Memoriam* and his glorious lines to Prince Albert.

'He was full of unbounded appreciation of beloved Albert. When he spoke of my own loss, of that of the Nation, his eyes quite filled with tears'. They shared a humorous moment when Tennyson talked of his Cockney invaders at Farringford. Her Majesty said she had no such trouble, and laughed at his riposte. 'Perhaps I should not be either if I could stick a sentry at my gates!'

Fig. 14. G. F. WATTS, *George Douglas Campbell, Eighth Duke of Argyll,* 1859-1860 (National Portrait Gallery).

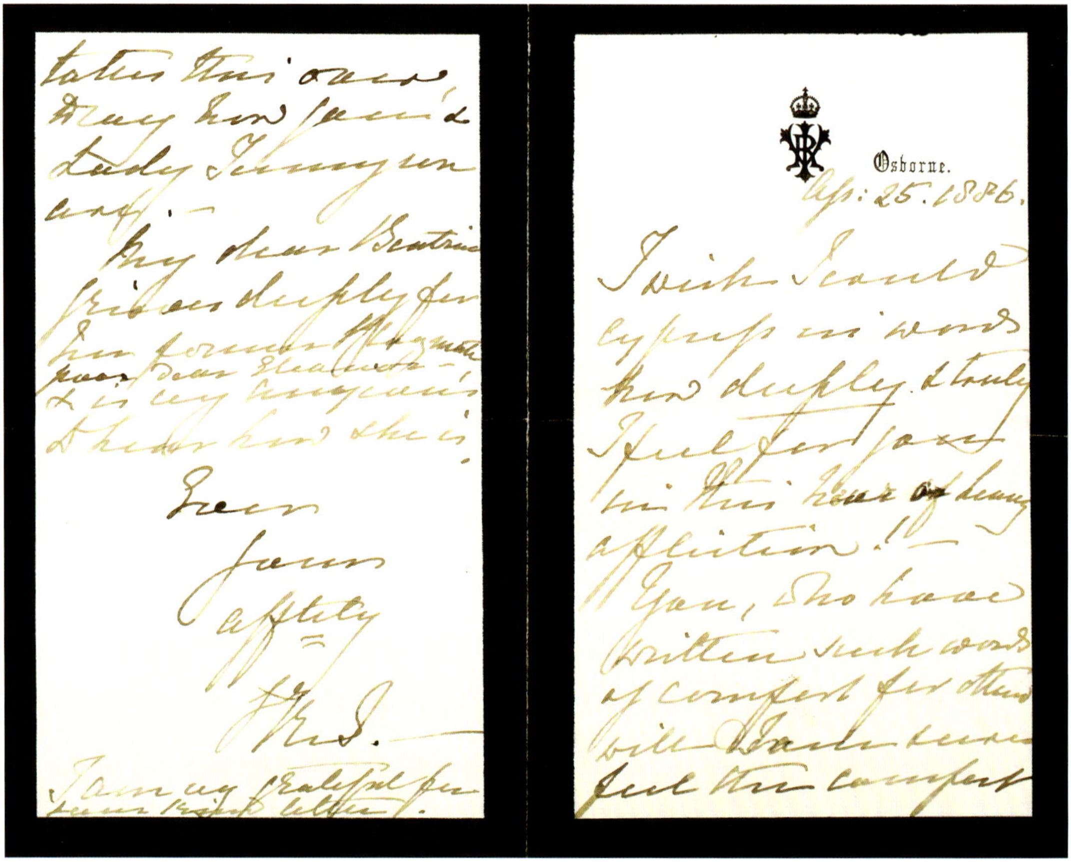
Osborne.
Apr: 25. 1886.

I wish I could express in words how deeply & truly I feel for you in this hour of heavy affliction! — You, who have written such words of comfort for others will I trust feel the comfort

taken thus once, may now you & Lady Tennyson [illegible] —

My dear Beatrice grieves deeply for her former playmate poor dear Eleanor — & is very anxious to hear how she is.

Ever yours affly V.R.I. —

I am very grateful for your kind letter.

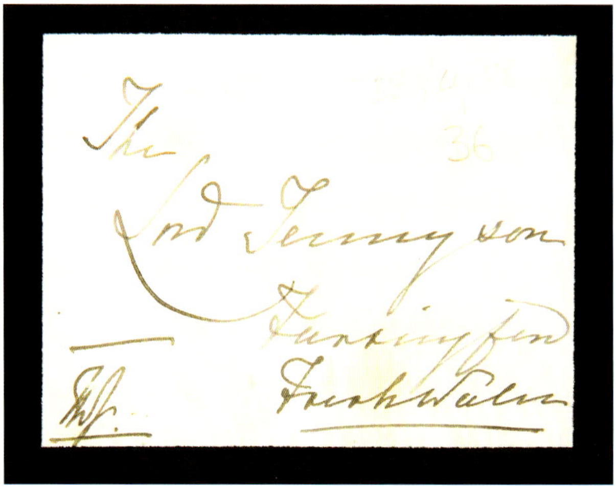
The Lord Tennyson
Farringford
Freshwater

36

48. *Letter to Alfred, Lord Tennyson,* 25 April 1886
7 ⅛ x 4 ½ inches, 18 x 11.3 cm, folded
ink on paper
TRC 4836

When the poet faced bereavement, the illness and death at sea of his younger son Lionel from a fever caught in India, Queen Victoria wrote heartfelt letters to him at Farringford:

> I wish I could express in words how *deeply* & truly I feel for you in this hour of heavy affliction! –
> You, who have written such words of comfort for others will I am sure feel the comfort of them again soon yourself. But it is *terrible* when one's grown up children, when one is no longer young oneself & to see, as I have done - & as *you* will do now – the sore stricken young Widow of one's beloved son!
> I will not weary you or intrude in your grief – by words of lamentation, which in fact – *can* offer none! But I say from the depth of a heart which has suffered cruelly - & lost almost all it cared for & loved best – I *feel* for you, I know what you & your dear Wife – are suffering.
> And I pray God to support you . . .
> Ever
Your
afftely
= / VRI
> I am very grateful for your kind letter

49. *Letter to Alfred, Lord Tennyson,* 9 August 1889
6 ⅞ x 4 ½ inches, 17.5 x 11.5 cm, folded
ink on paper
TRC 4839

The queen writes warmly to congratulate the poet laureate on his eightieth birthday, with news of her eldest grandson Wilhelm, Emperor of Germany, and the cordial relations between their two countries

> Though 3 days late, I hope I may still offer my best wishes for your 80 birthday & my hope that many more anniversaries may follow!
> My tie has been so much taken up by my Grandson, the Emperor of German's visit that I have hardly been able to write but my thoughts were with you on a day which is dear to me from being the birthday of my second Son & Son-in-law Ld Lorne.
> My grandson the Emperor of German's visit went off very well & much cordiality between the two countries was shown on both sides.
> Trusting that you are now quite recovered from your long illness
> Believe me always
> Yours
afftly
VRI
> Pray remember me to Lady Tennyson

G.F. Watts
1879.

GEORGE FREDERIC WATTS, OM RA (1817-1904)

Like Tennyson, George Frederic Watts, a friend of the poet laureate for four decades, aimed to elevate the nation through his art. He presented his portraits of leaders of the Victorian era to the opening of the National Portrait Gallery in 1896 and the Symbolist series he described as 'painted poems', to the opening of the National Gallery of British Art (Tate) in 1897.

Watts, having studied at Behnes's sculpture studio and briefly at the Royal Academy Schools, exhibited at the Royal Academy from 1837, the year Queen Victoria ascended the throne. After winning a top prize in the 1843 Palace of Westminster competition he spent three years in Florence as the protégé of the British Minister Lord Holland, painting frescoes and distinguished portrait commissions. He returned to England with a vision to fill a hall with frescos on the Progress of the Cosmos, Time and Civilization, these highly imaginative subjects – 'painted poems' – formed the nucleus of his Tate gift.

Tennyson met Watts in the 1850s at the Cosmopolitan Club, 'the Arcanum and the Parnassus of literary swells', who gathered in the artist's Mayfair studio. Visiting London, the poet often stayed at 'the Enchanted Palace', Little Holland House, where Watts lived as the tenant of Thoby and Sara Prinsep. Tennyson, who appears as the Cretan king Minos in Watts's fresco *Justice: A Hemicycle of Lawgivers* at Lincolns Inn (1853-1859), sat for six portraits over half a century, and after his death, Watts sculpted a memorial statue of the poet with his wolfhound (fig. 21).

At Freshwater, the artist stayed with Julia Margaret Cameron at Dimbola to paint portraits of the Tennysons and brought his young bride Ellen Terry. In 1874 he built The Briary, near Farringford. Here he brought his second wife Mary, who had posed for a Tennysonian photograph by. Mrs. Cameron.

Fig. 15. G. F. Watts, *Freshwater in Spring*, 1874 (Courtesy of the Fine Art Society).

50. *Alfred Tennyson* 1862-1864
oil on canvas
23 ½ x 19 ½ inches
60 x 49.5 cm
Private collection

As when a painter, poring on a face, Divinely through all hindrance finds the man
Behind it, and so paints him that his face,
The shape and colour of a mind and life,
Lives for his children, ever at its best
And fullest ('Lancelot and Elaine')

The first time Tennyson sat to Watts, he asked what was in his mind when painting a portrait and famously incorporated the artist's response into his idyll 'Lancelot and Elaine', uniting the spirit of poet and artist. Emily felt that the first portrait of 1858 (National Gallery of Victoria, Melbourne) did not capture his higher spirit. Not that she was seeking a particular expression, 'I *only* want what has scarcely yet been given in the world, the man at his highest stamp forever so long as canvas will last', she wrote to Woolner. The well-known contemplative 'moonlight' portrait of 1859 (Eastnor Castle) won her approval, as 'beautiful and touching'.

This rarely seen full-face portrait, commissioned by the ophthalmic surgeon William Bowman (later Sir William Bowman, president of the Ophthalmological Society) for 100 guineas and begun at Farringford on 29 November 1862, looked to Emily two days later, 'very grand'. Watts so enjoyed her bread and cheese at Farringford that she had a loaf sent down to Mrs. Cameron for him. He was painting two almost identical portraits at this time, the other he preserved for the national collection. Both present a stronger, more haunting image of Tennyson, who is seen against a symbolic background of poet's laurel - perhaps from a bush at Farringford - and the sea and changing sky. Bowman, 'delighted to hear you propose soon to finish for me the head of the great poet. The sooner the better', commissioned a self portrait. The idea was to have Watts and Tennyson hanging side by side as 'a *pair* of nobles answering one to the other on my walls' Bowman wrote on 17 November 1863. To his chagrin, they were different in handling and size. the three-quarter profile self-portrait of Watts in his wideawake hat (Tate, 1863-1864), an inch larger all round, faces the viewer, whereas the perhaps more powerful portrait of the poet shows him deep in thought.

Watts returned to Freshwater to paint a portrait of Tennyson for Trinity College, Cambridge, in 1890, when he painted a further portrait of the ennobled laureate in ermine (Adelaide, Art Gallery of South Australia).

204

51. *Portrait of Emily, Lady Tennyson,* 1862
oil on canvas
24 x 21¾ inches, 63.5 x 53.5 cm
The Collection: Art and Archaeology in Lincolnshire (Usher Gallery, Lincoln)

Emily Tennyson began sitting for her portrait on 21 November 1862, as a surprise gift for her husband. She found the artist so pleasant that time flew by. Hallam and Lionel were so interested in watching the procedure that 'they beg not to go out'.

Watts's habit was to have five or six two-hour sittings, lightly outlining the shape and starting with a detailed study of the face. While waiting for Emily's face to dry, he took the canvas back to Mrs. Cameron's cottage to work on detail and sent her servant up to Farringford. 'Will you kindly send by the bearer the lace veil you wore and the collar if it is not a fixture. The face of the picture is not dry enough to work upon but I can put in all the rest before I bring it for the last sitting, or rather another sitting'. The Duke and Duchess of Argyll, staying at Farringford when the finished portrait arrived on 24 June 1863, thought it looked like a Gainsborough. 'This is one of the great pictures that future generations will look at'. Another guest, Lady Grant, thought the portrait a speaking likeness. 'I do not know how such a beautiful picture has come', Emily wrote to Watts, 'You are a subtle alchemist, a great magician'. The artist, delighted, though as ever, wincing at exaggerated praise, added, 'Some of these days, I must try what I can make of Lionel, and that shall be for you all for yourself'.

52. *Portrait of Hallam and Lionel Tennyson,* 1865
oil on canvas
26 x 21 inches, 66 x 54 cm
The Collection: Art and Archaeology in Lincolnshire (Usher Gallery, Lincoln)

In the event, two years later Watts painted both boys. 'Mrs Cameron writes to Mr Prinsep that you have expressed a desire that I should paint your boys before they lose the glory of their locks', the artist wrote to Emily on 25 February 1865. Hallam and Lionel were to have their golden hair cut for school. The artist asked to wait until Easter, when he would happily start the portrait. 'The price shall be the pride I shall feel in giving pleasure to so great a man as Alfred Tennyson should I happily succeed, ... & the satisfaction of having done my best with that object should I be so unfortunate as to fail'. Emily was clearly concerned about timing because Watts begged that their hair-cutting be left till the last'. Sittings began on 10 April – Good Friday fell on 14th. Hallam stands on the right, facing the viewer, as he usually did in photographs. Emily's private thought in October, that the painting was 'very beautiful but not so beautiful as they. Like them but not their very selves', is fair. The artist's strength was in expressing the inner mind, the thought behind the face. As Tennyson later observed to the American poet Henry Wadsworth Longfellow, 'Those are my boys when they were girls'.

52A. ALFRED TENNYSON
Letter to Hallam Tennyson, (nd, probably 29 April 1857)
6 x 3 ⅝ inches, 15.4 x 9.3 cm
TRC: 8158

53. *Self-Portrait*, 1879
oil on canvas
66 x 53.3 cm, 26 x 21 cm,
Watts Gallery, COMWG 9

Watts was seen as the old master in the modern man. In this self-portrait of 1879, the year the Uffizi Gallery in Florence honoured Watts with an invitation to contribute to their gallery of self-portraits, the artist stands proud and contemplative in his painting smock, in profile before a rich red curtain, the colour that appealed to both poet and artist. Watts wears the deep red velvet skullcap made for him by Anne Prinsep in 1874. His emulation of Titian in art and manner gave rise to the nickname 'Signor' by which he was known to the Tennysons, Prinseps, Julia Margaret Cameron and all close friends.

At the time of painting, Watts had embarked on a series of literary polemics, published in the erudite *Nineteenth Century* journal edited by the poet's friend and architect [Sir] James Knowles; and his metaphysical paintings, exhibited at the opening of the avant-garde Grosvenor Gallery in London and the 1878 Exposition Universelle in Paris, and highlighted by Oscar Wilde, were attracting widespread interest and controversy. His contributions to the Grosvenor in 1879 were two ravishing literary and mythological pictures of *Paolo and Francesca* and *Orpheus and Euridyce,* a portrait of the prime minister William Ewart Gladstone and *Enid and Geraint*, a tribute to Julia Margaret Cameron's illustration to Tennyson's *Idylls*.

54. *Portrait of Henry Thoby Prinsep* (1792-1878), 1871
oil on canvas
20 x 16 inches, 51 x 41 cm
Watts Gallery: COMWG 153

The warmth and vigour of Watts's friendship with Thoby Prinsep can be seen in this, the best of several portraits of his erudite companion. A member of the Council of India, he was a wonderful larger-than-life figure, with an encyclopaedic memory. Tennyson, too, enjoyed his erudite companionship, although he was not best pleased when Signor and Thoby purchased fields next door to Farringford in the autumn of 1864. By the time Watts had commissioned the Arts and Crafts architect Philip Webb to build The

Briary in 1872, as Little Holland House was to be demolished, the artist was relieved to find Tennyson more encouraging. 'I am glad you think my house will not disfigure the neighbourhood of Farringford,' Watts wrote on 28 December.

Tennyson used to walk over to The Briary almost daily to read to Thoby Prinsep, whose eyesight was failing, was very much an invalid. Anny Thackeray recalled that 'Mr Prinsep wears a long veil and a high coned hat and quantities of coats. When he was fit to walk with Tennyson and Watts, people in Freshwater used to stop and stare as the three men passed by in their distinctive hats and cloaks.

Fig. 16. *Sara Prinsep*, 1850 (detail, Watts Gallery). To Tennyson, she was the ' Principessa' of Little Holland House.

VISITORS TO FARRINGFORD

'Everybody is either a genius, or a poet, or a painter or peculiar in some way', wrote Anny Thackeray on a visit to Freshwater in 1865. Her friend wondered 'Is there nobody commonplace? As the residence of the poet laureate, Freshwater was a Mecca for intellectuals, keen to talk to him. It was compared to a French *salon* or Athens in the age of Pericles. Leaders of Victorian society, poets, painters and philosophers crossed the Solent and headed for Farringford. Not all were welcome to the poet. While Tennyson was a splendid host to friends who liked to walk, learn nature's secrets, large and small, to gaze at the stars and listen to his poetry recital; strangers, 'Cockneys' as he referred to tourists who invaded his privacy, were given short shrift.

The poet's closest friends on the Isle of Wight were the member of parliament Sir John Simeon and Julia Margaret Cameron, who took up photography in 1864. Among other early visitors to Farringford were Prince Albert (cats. 3 and 48), the artist Richard Doyle (fig. 2), the artist, musician and author of Nonsense stories, Edward Lear (cats. 7, 8 and 30) and the writer and photographer the Reverend Charles Dodgson 'Lewis Carroll' (cat. 62), the Pre-Raphaelite artists William Holman Hunt and John Everett Millais (figs. 6 and 13), the Duke of Argyll (fig. 14), and Frederic Denison Maurice (cat. 56), founding father of the Cambridge Apostles, of the Working Men's College and Queen's College and godfather to Hallam. Professor Benjamin Jowett, Master of Balliol (cat. 57), used to visit yearly and the actress Ellen Terry (cats. 60, 61 and 69), came to Farringford during her few months of marriage to Watts in 1864, the year Garibaldi famously planted a Wellingtonia (fig. 5 and cats. 58. and 59). Queen Emma of the Sandwich Islands (cat. TF.10 and fig. 22) had a special chair carved for her at Farringford in 1865. The American poet Henry Wadsworth Longfellow (cat. 72), young Prince Alamayou of Abyssinia (cat. 70) came in 1868, the year the young Mary Fraser Tytler (cats. 70-71 and 79), future second wife of G. F. Watts, modelled for the Tennysons' closest friend and neighbour Julia Margaret Cameron. The artist Helen Allingham painted a series of pictures of Farringford (fig. 4), the estate (cat. 9) and the poet himself (cat. 42) in the latter part of his life.

55. '*Famous Visitors to Farringford*'
pen and ink
19⅜ x 11 ¼ inches, 49.3 x 18.5 cm
TRC: 5475

56. LOWES CATO DICKINSON (1819-1908)
Frederic Denison Maurice (1805-1872), 1886
chalk on grey paper, highlighted with white
14 x 10 inches, 35 x 25 cm
Inscribed 'F. D. M. / 1859 / B. 1903 D.1872 /
Lowes Dickinson fecit'
Kings College, London

The Christian Socialist Frederick Denison Maurice,
godfather to Hallam Tennyson, was the founder of
the Working Men's College and of Queen's College.
This fine drawing, one of several replicas, made on
Maurice's death by Lowes Dickinson, from his 1859
pastel portrait (Trinity College, Cambridge) –
notably, for the Working Men's College and
Queen's – is a recent gift to King's College,
London. After Maurice's resignation in October
1853 from his professorship at Kings, Tennyson
wrote a poem of support for Maurice in January
1854, inviting him to Farringford. When he visited
in 1858, Emily wrote 'I never saw anyone, except
perhaps one, who seemed so to commune with the
Most High'.

To the Rev. F.D. Maurice'

Come, when no graver cares employ,
Godfather, come and see your boy:
   Your presence will be sun in winter,
Making the little one leap for joy.

For, being of that honest few,
Who give the Fiend himself his due,
   Should eighty-thousand college-councils
Thunder 'Anathema,' friend, at you;

Should all our churchmen foam in spite
At you, so careful of the right,
   Yet one lay-hearth would give you welcome
(Take it and come) to the Isle of Wight;

Where, far from noise and smoke of town,
I watch the twilight falling brown
   All round a careless-order'd garden
Close to the ridge of a noble down.

You'll have no scandal while you dine,
But honest talk and wholesome wine,
   And only hear the magpie gossip
Garrulous under a roof of pine:

For groves of pine on either hand,
To break the blast of winter, stand;
   And further on, the hoary Channel
Tumbles a billow on chalk and sand;

 . . . Come, Maurice, come: the lawn as yet
Is hoar with rime, or spongy-wet;
   But when the wreath of March has blossom'd,
Crocus, anemone, violet,

Or later, pay one visit here,
For those are few we hold as dear;
   Nor pay but one, but come for many,
Many and many a happy year. *January, 1854.*

57. GEORGE RICHMOND
(1809-1896)
Professor Benjamin Jowett
(1817-93), c1855
pencil and chalk on paper
24 x 18 inches, 61 x 45.8 cm
Balliol College, Oxford

Benjamin Jowett, the Master of Balliol from 1870 to 1893, was the Regius Professor of Greek at Oxford when George Richmond made this drawing. Jowett visited Farringford every Christmas for 40 years, from 1853.

In 1855, Tennyson supported Jowett when his radical essay on atonement in *The Epistles of St Paul* was attacked. It was then that Richmond, whose son was at Exeter College, Oxford, made the present drawing, which remained in his family collection. Jowett too praised *Maud*, writing that even in Shakespeare no 'ecstasy of love soars to such a height'.

Jowett, whom Allingham described as frank, yet cautious, 'a soft smooth round man, with . . . a very gentle voice and manner', would suggest subjects for poems. In January 1861, he found that Tennyson had been suffering from depression, and needed encouragement. 'This year he has written nothing but a short piece called 'Boadicea', in a very wild peculiar metre, with long lines and innumerable short syllables. It is very fine, but too strange to be popular'. The laureate clearly disliked Byron, but enjoyed discussing Wordsworth over a pipe. ' I respect his character, notwithstanding a superficial irritability and uneasiness about all things . . . he is so greatly mistaken by those who don't know him', wrote Jowett. 'No one is more honest, truthful, manly, or a warmer friend; but he is as open as the day.' In later years, Jowett used to sit by the fire at Farringford, while he translated of Plato (1871). At Freshwater, he also sat to Watts and for a splendid photograph by Julia Margaret Cameron.

58. GEORGE FREDERIC WATTS
Giuseppe Garibaldi, 1864
oil on canvas
28 ¾ x 21 ⅛ inches, 73 x 53.6 cm
Private Collection

59. GIUSEPPE GARIBALDI (1807-1882)
after UGO FOSCOLO (1778-1827) *'L'orne dei forti'*
ink on paper, inscribed *To my friend Alfred Tennyson / G. Garibaldi'*
5 ⅝ x 8 inches, 14.5 x 20.3 cm
TRC

General Giuseppe Garibaldi (1807-82) came to England in April 1864 to drum up support for the unification of Italy. Crowds surged to greet the Italian hero, whose visit on 5 April was the event of the year at Farringford. A commanding figure in his white poncho and red lining, Garibaldi wore the embroidered red shirt outlined here by Watts. The *Illustrated London News* highlighted the Tennyson family greeting the general as he stepped under the portico, still slightly wounded, with the aid of a stick (fig. 5).

'What a noble human being! I expected to see a hero and I was not disappointed', Tennyson wrote to the Duke of Argyll: 'He is more majestic than meek, and his manners have a certain divine simplicity in them, such as I have never witnessed in a native of these islands, among men at least, and they are gentler than those of most young maidens whom I know'. Islanders, who had wait two hours for his arrival, rushed forward to shake his hand. Garibaldi stood up and bowed.

Tennyson took him up into his study. 'He came here and smoked his cigar in my little room and we had a half hour's talk in English', the poet recalled. 'I doubt whether he understood me perfectly, and his meaning was often obscure to me. I ventured to give him a little advice: he denied that he came with any political purpose to England'. He said he had come to thank the English for their kindness and the interest in Italy, and to consult an English specialist about his leg. They read poetry to each other. Garibaldi's choice was Ugo Foscolo's *L'orne dei Forti* (cat. 53), which he wrote out for the poet and received in return a copy of *Idylls of the King*. Afterwards, the Tennysons introduced him to the poet Sir Henry Taylor and others. It is wonderful to envisage the usually indomitable Julia Margaret Cameron falling to her knees, thrusting up her chemical-stained hands and begging to photograph and immortalize his heroic Italian soul. Garibaldi mistook her for a beggar and refused. He then ceremoniously planted a wellingtonia on the lawn. It had been presented by his London hostess, the Duchess of Sutherland.

At Stafford House, artists pursued Garibaldi with their sketchbooks. His tight schedule could not accommodate portrait sittings, but as her son Lord Gower, reminisced, 'An exception, however, was made in favour of a very great artist Watts'. Like Tennyson, Watts admired the Italian's campaign for Italian freedom and the duchess arranged sittings for seven until eight in the morning, only to find on arrival Garibaldi absent. He promised the duchess to be available the next day. Anxious not to let Watts down again, she herself went to the dining-room at seven to find the General and a trio of artists hard at work, but no Watts. *'Mais je ne vois pas mon artiste'*, the duchess exclaimed – French was presumably the language they understood better than each other's. *'Mais, Madame, il me semble qu'il y en a trois ici'*, replied Garibaldi. Watts soon arrived.

Although Mary Watts notes in *George Frederic Watts: The Annals of an Artist's Life* that as he painted this head study, the sitter was receiving deputations and sitting patiently as the duchess read aloud, Garibaldi appears engaged, motivated, the head strong. Despite curtailed sittings that could not enable a finished portrait – the mystical study at Watts Gallery did not satisfy the artist – this sketch captures the compelling aura of Garibaldi.

60. (DAME ALICE) ELLEN TERRY (1847-1928)
Letter to Hallam, Lord Tennyson, (postmark 22 March 1893)
ink on paper
8 x 1 inches, 20 x 12.5 cm
TRC: 7012

The actress, starring as 'Rosalind' opposite Henry Irving as 'Becket' in the title role of Alfred, Lord Tennyson's play at the Lyceum Theatre, London, reminisces to Hallam after the laureate's death, about their young days at Farringford in 1864, when she was the bride of G. F. Watts (cat. 68).

> I have wondered sometimes whether you remember me as a girl at Freshwater, & whether you were there when I bumbled off the gate in the grand excitement of a paper-chase? Lionel took a great splinter out of my wrist – I recollect – I was 17 in years then, but scarcely 7, in wisdom / I fear = It's about 27 years ago but I remember it all vividly - & remember yr mother as she looked then – like an exquisite Tea-Rose –

61. ELLEN WARDELL (DAME ALICE ELLEN TERRY)
Letter to Hallam Tennyson, 7 January 1881
6 x 3 ¾ inches, 15 x 9.5 cm
TRC 4360

Ellen Terry, soon to part from her second husband, the lesser actor Charles 'Kelly' Wardell, had opened 'Camma' in Tennyson's *The Cup* opened on 3 January. Now at the height of her fame, Ellen has received a letter from the poet laureate, of whom she is still in awe. She signs herself in character, underlining her words with characteristic thespian emphasis:

> <HE HE> has written to me – not Linnatus, but your Father - & such a letter! I shd feel honester if I didn't know his commendation comes <u>before</u> his knowledge of what I am able to do – but "some have greatness thrust upon them" & I most assuredly know that I have not "achieved" – deserved?) – this letter from him – He has taken me upon faith – "Common Report is a common liar", & I dread his coming on Saturday – or any day =
> I don't think he'll like <u>any of it!</u> Except Henry Irving's <u>acting</u> – Don't you think that extraordinarily clever? I do. Synorix is so unlike H.I. it is such a bit of <u>acting. That night</u> has left its reflection in lines in my face & pains in my back =
> Greeting & health from Camma to your grand Father -= I could not write to him – I dare not . . . + Will you give him my love & thanks & say for me what I <u>should</u> say, if I could -

62. THE REV. CHARLES LUTWIDGE DODGSON 'LEWIS CARROLL' (1832-1898)
Letter to Alfred Tennyson, 19 June 1872
ink on paper
7 x 4 ½ inches, 17.7 x 11.2 cm
TRC 6764

Charles Dodgson, the photographer and author of *Alice's Adventures in Wonderland* (1865), and shortly before that of *Through the Looking Glass* (1871), writes to recommend a Sheffield doctor to help cure Lionel's stammer.

Dodgson first met and photographed Tennyson and his 'most beautiful boys' in the Lake District in 1857. Staying at Plumbley's Hotel in Freshwater in April 1859, he came to Farringford one morning and returned in the afternoon for six-year-old Hallam to sign his photograph. Communications with the poet faltered when Dodgson wrote for permission to read an unpublished manuscript, 'The Window', which Tennyson had circulated to closer friends. More than once, Dodgson unintentionally upset the poet and his wife. In their absence on 13 - 18 August 1874, he took a series of photographs of their staff and extended family at Farringford, photographing the house itself on the 17th.

63. VALENTINE CAMERON PRINSEP, RA (1838-1904)
Audrey Boyle, c 1883-1884
oil on canvas
36 x 28 inches, 91.4 x 71 cm
Private collection

Hallam Tennyson's fiancée Audrey Boyle gave various portrait sittings for Valentine Prinsep, second son of Thoby and Sara Prinsep (cat. 54), very likely as engagement portraits. Another shows Audrey reading a letter or poem on Afton down at Freshwater, while seagulls fly about. Her appreciation of Tennyson's poetry had won Hallam's heart. 'It all came to pass over In Memoriam', he wrote in October 1883 to Mary Gladstone, daughter of the prime minister. Hallam and Audrey were married at Westminster Abbey on 25 June 1884. Prinsep, who had trained with Watts before joining Rossetti and the Pre-Raphaelites painting Arthurian murals at the Oxford Union, went on to study at Gleyre's atelier in Paris 1859-1860. His large picture of The Delhi Durbar proclaiming Queen Victoria Empress of India was exhibited at the Royal Academy in 1880.

Fig. 17. Valentine Cameron Prinsep, *Audrey Tennyson on Afton Down*, c1883-1884.

JULIA MARGARET CAMERON
(1815-1879)

Julia Margaret Cameron, the only woman outside his family whom Tennyson addressed by her Christian name, moved to Freshwater in October 1860 to live near the poet she admired most, as her husband, the distinguished jurist Charles Hay Cameron, was often away in Ceylon. (Her other favoured poet wa Sir Henry Taylor).'This island might equal your island now for richness of effects', she enthused to Charles. 'The downs are covered with golden gorse & beneath them the blue hyacinth is so thickly opened that the valleys look as if the "sky were upbreaking thro' the Earth'". The Camerons bought two gabled cottages, which Julia later joined together and named Dimbola Lodge after Charles's coffee estate.

Julia was the most eccentric of the celebrated Pattle sisters, among them, Sara Prinsep. Passionately unconventional, they wore rich flowing robes that combined modern Parisian art with draperies of the High Renaissance and the Orient. Having been a prominent hostess in Calcutta, Julia brought her 'doubly distilled' energy, generosity and wit to Freshwater, where her eyes flashed, softened and sparkled as she sparred with Tennyson, or lured the sleeping poet to gaze at the moonlit sea for the good of his soul and poetry, pressing 'Golgotha mines' of gifts on to Emily.

The great gift to posterity was the camera given by her son-in-law Charles Norman for Christmas 1863 to occupy Julia in her husband's absence. Tennyson supported her enterprise, posing again and again and enticing eminent friends to her glasshouse studio. Julia Cameron registered, exhibited and signed her large soft-focus albumen prints 'From Life'. With Watts on hand to give artistic advice, the poet, his family and, famously, his *Idylls of the King*, she threw her energy into creating photographs of international renown, a vibrant legacy of the spirit of the Victorian era.

Fig. 18. Oscar Gustave Rejlander, *Julia Margaret Cameron At her Piano*, 1863 (modern print).

64. *Letter to Hallam Tennyson*, 15 March 1856
ink on paper
7 x 4 ½ inches, 17.7 x 11.5 cm, folded
TRC 3498

Julia Cameron's letter to the poet's three-year-old son Hallam shows her affection for the poet's family and poetry, her deep religious fervour, aesthetic appreciation and maternal warmth. She refers to three of her six children, Julia, who married Charles Norman, donor of the camera, Charles Hay Cameron and Henry Hirschel Hay Cameron who would later establish a photographic studio in London. It was through her friendship with William Hirschel (1792-1871), president of the Royal Astronomical Society, as well as a lesson with David Wilkie Wynfield (1837-1887), that Julia Cameron had learned to master the science of photography

My darling little Hallam

I have not forgotten that your birthday is come again. May God bless it to you my sweet little one and make it to come often and often finding you "growing in stature and favour with God and Man" which means getting tall & great like Papa & Mama – praying to be good – and trying to be beloved ————-

I have been thinking a great deal about what is the nicest thing I could send you as a "Birthday present" from "Mrs Tameron" who loves you dearly and I decided that next to the Bible there was no book likely to be dear to you and few more good for you than your own beloved Papa's beautiful Poetry – therefore I thought you would like to have it all, *as all your own* and I have put the Books into green dresses – like the green dress you liked so much when you wished to be a Leaf & to go & live up in the Tree with me? Do you remember darling - ?

I remember well all the happy days spent in your dear house – and I wish with all my heart I was going to spend your Birthday with you. Will you give your Mama one of your largest longest kisses for me, and Juley: do you remember that happy romping girl Juley? And do you remember what good romps you used to have with "Mrs Tameron. I hope your Books will arrive without having the edges scratched & rubbed – I was obliged to leave the edges open as it is a post office rule – and I was obliged to send them by post as it is the only way by which I can be sure to get them to your dear Mama's hand without trouble –

How I wish when my little Charlie and Henry are playing that they were playing with you and darling little Lionel you would be four such happy little people and such *great little* friends. But I hope these happy days will come.

My love and kisses to you & your little Brother & love to Papa and Mama from "Mrs Cameron".

65. *The Dirty Monk*, 1865
albumen print
15 x 12 inches
38 x 30.4 cm
Julia Margaret
Cameron
Trust,
Dimbola

'Julia Cameron, Julia Cameron, you are a dreadful woman', Tennyson exclaimed as the photographer came flying up to Farringford in a carriage specially hired to transport her huge sheaf of photographs for his signature. She would plump them down on his table, with a range of new pens so that the laureate would have no excuse not to sign the photographs. *The Dirty Monk*, as Tennyson titled this image, was his favourite of the many photographs she took of him.

66. *Alfred Tennyson*, 1867
albumen print
13 x 10 inches,
33 x 25.2 cm
Farringford
Estate

Travelling back to the Isle of Wight in 1867, William Allingham saw her on the train sitting 'queenly' in a carriage all to herself, surrounded by albumen prints. 'I want to do a large photograph of Tennyson, and he objects! Says I make bags under his eyes.' She was struggling to persuade Carlyle to sit for what became a masterpiece, '*Carlyle like a rough block of Michael Angelo's Sculpture*. 'He says it is a kind of *Inferno!* The *greatest* men of the age, Sir John Herschel, Henry Taylor, Watts, say I have *immortalised* them – and these other men object!! What is one to do – Hm?' The present photograph is testament to Julia Cameron's persuasive powers. Tennyson complained to her that thanks to her photographs, he could not go unrecognised 'by reason of your confounded photographs'.

67. *Sir John Simeon Bt,* registered 1870
albumen
13⅛ x 10 ⅛ inches
33.5 x 260 cm
Private Collection

Sir John Simeon (1815-1870) was Tennyson's closest friend on the Isle of Wight. The squire of Swainston Hall at Calbourne, some eight miles east of Freshwater, he was member of parliament for the island and master of the foxhounds. His fresh, cultivated nature, humorous and sincere added zest to the poet's life. It was at Simeon's encouragement that Tennyson developed *Maud* (cats. 32-33), and when he died, the poet wrote 'In the Garden at Swainston' in memory of his friend.

'He was the Prince of Courtesy. The only man on earth, I verily believe, to whom I could, and more than once opened my whole heart, ' the poet wrote to Lady Simeon. 'He has also given me, in many a conversation at Farringford, in my little attic, his utter confidence. I knew none like him for tenderness and generosity.'

68. *George Frederic Watts*, 1865
15 x 11 ⅝ inches
38.3 x 29.5 cm
TRC 5480

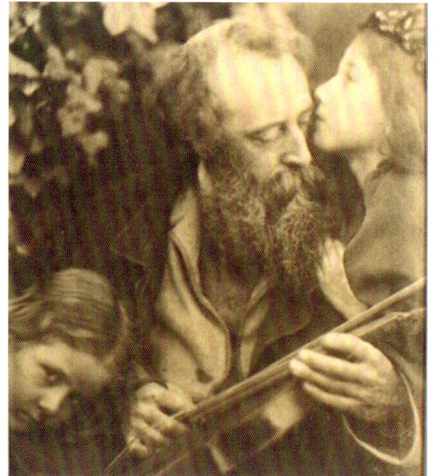

Fig. 19. The *Whisper of the Muse*,
1865.

69. *Ellen Terry*, 1864
albumen
9 ½ x 7 ½ inches,
24 x 19 cm
private collection

G. F. Watts brought seventeen-year-old actress Ellen Terry (1847-1928) to Farringford shortly after their marriage on 20 February 1864. This freshly discovered photograph shows his bride in her brown silk wedding dress designed by the Pre-Raphaelite artist William Holman Hunt. Julia Cameron had recently acquired her camera. Ellen is the first of Watts's sitters she photographed, momentously modelling for her bridal portrait *Choosing* (National Portrait Gallery), in which she is seen choosing between the fragrant violets of love she holds to her breast, and the exotic camellia all about her symbolizing the theatre. Ellen has hardly moved; she has just brought one hand down to the other. In contrast to Watts's exquisite portrait, where it is the artist who is doubtful, Cameron's photograph shows the teenager's anxiety. It is a remarkably honest picture of Ellen, almost spontaneous – though sitting to Mrs. Cameron was an arduous affair. Who is Ellen watching? She is longing to move, to take part, act. How this photograph contrasts with the refined beauty and pathos of Cameron's well-known photograph *Sadness*, which until now was thought to have been photographed at Farringford. Ellen recorded on her cabinet card of *Sadness* that it had been taken on her seventeenth birthday, in 'the cottage' belonging to Julia's sister Maria Jackson.

Soon afterwards, Ellen arrived at Farringford, to find the poet laureate sitting here at his library table. Emily was standing on a step-ladder, her hands protected by thick gloves as she handed heavy books down to him. She looked very frail, 'like a faint tea-rose, and spent most of the time lying on her crimson sofa. Ellen accompanied Tennyson on his evening walks, learning the different flight paths of each bird. The poet told her to watch the solid phalanxes turning against the sunset turning into a wedge shape and suddenly narrowing. He showed her how to recognize the barks of trees and wildflowers. Finding him 'wonderfully simple', she saw poetry in his every move and was 'mighty proud' when she learned how to prepare his long churchwarden pipe so that it did not stick to his lips. Impressed by his reading, Ellen loved the way he read Browning's 'How They Brought the Good News from Ghent to Aix making the words sound like hoofs' clattering along a road, but her greatest fun at Freshwater, as cat. 60 bears witness, was playing Indians and Knights of the Round Table with Hallam and Lionel and the Cameron children. Watts and Tennyson seemed very old, when 'my young knights were waiting for me'.

70. MARY FRASER TYTLER (1849-1938), after JULIA MARGARET CAMERON
Captain Speedy, Déjatch Alámayou and Básha Fliká
albumen and watercolour, 1868
in a decorative carte-de-visite album, signed on opposite folio
by Prince Alamayou and Captain Speedy
Watts Gallery

Tennyson arranged for seven-year-old Déjatch Alámayou, the orphaned son of Emperor Theodore II of Abyssinia to sit to Julia Cameron. After the emperor shot himself in April 1868 rather than surrender to the British at the Siege of Magdala, Queen Victoria invited the prince to England. Déjatch came to Farringford with his guardian Captain Tristram Speedy. As he was driven past the large ilex, the nervous prince called out, 'Take care: there will be an elephant in that jungle.'

Eighteen-year-old Mary Fraser Tytler was assisting the photographer on 23 July when Captain Tristram brought the prince to the studio. Déjatch wore western clothes in England, but Cameron dressed him and his entourage in Abyssinian costume for the sittings. The tiny unregistered print that Mary pasted into her album, not one of the ten registered by Mrs Cameron, may have been a trial photograph, unless Mary took it herself. Captain Speedy sits in an embroidered fez and lion-skin tippet, his arm around Déjatch, who is wearing a purple shirt and large ethnic necklace; Casa, the prince's attendant stands behind them with a shield made by Mary. She set the photograph in the Abyssinian jungle, drawing a tiger on a mountain ledge, chained to a coconut palm and protecting her cubs, with anklets ornamented with bells lying nearby, suggesting an escape.

Queen rose of the rosebud garden of girls,
  Come hither, the dances are done,
In gloss of satin and glimmer of pearls,
  Queen lily and rose in one;
Shine out, little head, sunning over with curls,
  To the flowers, and be their sun.

There has fallen a splendid tear
  From the passion-flower at the gate.
She is coming, my dove, my dear;
  She is coming, my life, my fate;
The red rose cries, "She is near, She is near;"
  And the white rose weeps, "She is late;"
The larkspur listens, "I hear, I hear;"
  And the lily whispers, "I wait."   *Maud*

71. *Rosebud Garden of Girls*, 1868
albumen
11 ¾ x 10 ¾ inches, 30 x 27.3cm
Private collection

Julia Cameron's meteoric success as an art photography pioneer gave her the confidence to attempt a group photograph to illustrate *Maud*. As sitters she chose the Fraser Tytler sisters, Etheldred, Christina, Mary and Eleanor, who were holidaying on the island. The girls had been to a dance at Farringford – 'Jolly fun,' thought Mary. Tennyson took her to see the blue crescent of Venus through a telescope. He read *Maud*, holding her hand to calm her nerves, and walked her down to marvel at the moonlit sea. It is no wonder, that Julia Cameron's symbolic photograph celebrating Tennyson's famous epic worked well, not least with the beautiful poet Christina, (centre left) and Mary (centre right), a highly imaginative artist.

Like Tennyson and Watts, Julia Margaret Cameron aimed to depict the soul of the age, to ennoble art by experiment, to create modern images of intense poetic beauty, with a high moral purpose.

The photographer draped climbing roses over a screen in her dining room to provide a virginal backdrop for *The Rosebud Garden of Girls*. She clearly looked to Dante Gabriel Rossetti's painting *The Beloved*, on exhibition two years earlier at the Arundel Club; and although the artist himself refused to face her lens, his brother William Michael Rossetti had been posing for her when he began the painting. Her attempt with a fifth girl focussing on Mary herself, failed. The composition was a mess and the backdrop slipped, leaving the dining-room curtains visible above the screen, but the photographer printed the image, took another which she later cropped to show only Christina, Eleanor and Ethel, renamed the group *The Three Sisters: Peace, Love and Faith*. At last, Mrs. Cameron achieved her ideal.

Julia Margaret Cameron used to say that no woman should allow herself to be photographed between the ages of 18 and 80, but in this Pre-Raphaelite group, each sister holding flowers from Maud's garden, only Eleanor was young enough. She stands on the left, with passion flowers at her shoulder; looking dreamily upwards at the viewer. Ethel, standing on the far right, has a spray of lilies in her hand and an apprehensive expression, 'I wait'. Ethereally poetic, sitting in the centre beside Mary, Christina, holds a red rose, symbol of martyrdom. Mary's strong jaw line seems to heighten her concentration as she looks down, a larkspur rising from the cluster of foliage and heart's tongue fern leaf stretched over her lap. Each girl seems to be absorbed in her role in the scene they are recreating to illustrate the combined genius of Cameron and Tennyson. The photographer has transmitted her profound sentiment to these unusually receptive sitters, who appreciated the Christian iconography and maidenly purity of their flowers. As well as *Maud*, there is a sense here also of *The Princess*. This print, given to the Fraser Tytlers, was inscribed by Christina 'No one in all the world [illegible] Mrs. Cameron challenges all Europe to produce from life a [illegible] equal to this'.

That day, the poet William Allingham invited for lunch at Dimbola, faced a riot of Fraser Tytlers dashing upstairs in fancy dress, followed by the triumphant photographer. She held the dripping glass negative up high, her hands black with collodion and exclaimed, 'Magnificent! To focus them all in one picture, such an effort!' Indeed it was. Julia Margaret Cameron sent a print to Rossetti, who found it 'full of beauty, but in so large a group the interference in some degree of unlucky natural accidents in the arrangement is quite impossible to be avoided. Among a bevy of beauties one does not know I should say from the photograph that Eleanor and Christina bear away the palm . . . over the beauty of general effect and arrangement you seem somehow to have acquired a degree of control quite your own.'

72. *Henry Wadsworth, Longfellow (1807-82)*, 1868
facsimile from cat. 37

The American poet Henry Wadsworth Longfellow came to Farringford with a party of ten on 15 July 1868. During this rare European tour, the celebrated author of *Hiawatha* was prevailed upon by the great and the good, from the Queen to the Archbishop of Canterbury and the novelist Charles Dickens; and he had agreed to sit to Watts.

Longfellow's sister recorded their experience driving through the narrow winding lanes, between stone walls overhung with ivy, or hedges of sweet briar – after which Watts's house The Briary was named – until they arrived at Farringford's simple gate. They drove through a long avenue of tall trees, winding their way up to the rambling mansion.

The Tennysons gave a tea party for some fifty guests to meet Longfellow. Emily, though floating around the garden in black herself, in mourning for her father, had placed brightly coloured shawls and rugs on the lawn so that her guests could relax. All were longing for a word with Longfellow, especially the women. To Tiny Cotton, though, his long silver hair, whiskers and beard and slick countenance made him appear venerable, but nothing like 'the furrowed lines of our bard'.

Longfellow was very taken with the Fraser Tytler girls, who had been playing croquet. Collapsing into a chair, he teased them about the English mania for croquet, and told his hosts that 'it was worth while coming to England to see such young ladies.'

Dropping into Orchard Brothers for tobacco, Tennyson took Longfellow to sit for his photograph at Dimbola, leaving the American with a warning, 'You will have to do whatever she tells you. I'll come back soon and see what is left of you.'

73. *Cecy, A Study*, 1871
albumen print
12 ¾ x 10 3/16 inches, 32.4 x 25.9 cm
TRC 5392

Cecilia 'Cecy' Tennyson (1859-1918), photographed at fifteen or sixteen, was one of the five children of Tennyson's youngest brother Horatio. After their mother died in 1868, Emily arranged for them to rent one of Julia Cameron's cottages, and organized a governess.

74. *'He thought of that sharp look Mother, I gave him yesterday'*, registered. 1 May 1875
albumen print
14 x 11 ½ inches, 35. 5x 29 cm
TRC: 5463

Lionel Tennyson poses with Emily Peacock to recreate Tennyson's 'May Queen (1833).
The photographer clearly worried about the shoes, as there is only one other known print.

75 ALFRED, LORD TENNYSON
'The Bugle Song' from *The Princess*, 'The Charge of the Light Brigade',
'The Charge of the Heavy Brigade', 'Ask Me No More', 'Northern Farmer, New Style', verses from *Maud*, 'Boadicea' and 'The Wellington Ode',
recording, 15 May 1890
Farringford Estate

76. *Graphic*, 15 October 1892
REGINALD CLEAVER,
'Lord Tennyson and his Nurse on Freshwater Down',
Annabel Watts Collection

77. HALLAM, LORD TENNYSON
Album on the publication of *Alfred Lord Tennyson, A Memoir by his Son* , London Macmillan, 1897 (with letters of congratulation from Prime Ministers, William Ewart Gladstone, the Earl of Rosebery and the Marquess of Salisbury)
Farringford Estate

Fig. 20. 'The Choice and Master Spirits of this Age: 'Poet and the Painter: Mr G F Watts RA, Painting Lord Tennyson's Portrait in the Poet Laureate's study, at Freshwater', *Daily Graphic*, 8 September 1891

78. WALTER FIELD
(1837-1901)
Tennyson's Russian Wolfhound, 1900
pencil and watercolour on grey paper,
6 ½ x 10 inches,
16.5 x 25.4 cm
Private Collection

Fig. 21. G. F. Watts, *Memorial to Alfred Lord Tennyson*, 1898-1903, Lincoln.

Walter Field, who knew Alfred and Emily at Shiplake, where they were married, drew his Russian wolfhound Karenina at Farringford in the first week of May 1900. Field inscribed the picture 'Tennyson's favourite old Russian wolfhound . . . Seventeen years old – very old for her breed. Karenina is the dog seen in Watts's memorial statue of Tennyson at Lincoln. The borzoi, as this breed is now known, is an aristocratic dog, sensitive, graceful, alert, aloof and quick as lighting.

Tennyson seems to have owned several dogs at the end of his life, an Irish deerhound Lufra, a terrier Winks (fig. 12) as well as Karenina. When Watts returned to Farringford in May 1890 to paint his last two portraits of the poet laureate, one in doctoral robes for Trinity College, Cambridge (figs. 7 and 20) and the other in his peer's robes (Adelaide), Mary Watts walked up to meet the artist and poet. 'Down the great aisle of elms they came, a white Russian deerhound flashing like silver through the sun or shade, and the central figure the poet, a note of black in the midst of vivid green, grand in the folds of his ample cloak and his face looming grandly from the shadow of the giant hat.'

79. MARY SETON WATTS (1849-1938)
Sundial, 1907-1908
Terracotta
Farringford estate

Mary Seton Watts, designer of the Watts Chapel in Compton, Surrey and founder of the Compton Potters' Arts Guild, had known the Tennysons since 1868 (cat. 70). Hallam had invited her to accompany her husband back to Farringford for his portraits of the poet in 1890. Her medal-winning garden ornaments were shown in landmark Liberty & Co exhibitions from 1903 and exhibited for Ireland at the 1904 World's Fair in St. Louis, U.S.A.

On 15 February 1907, Mary wrote to Hallam that she was designing a sundial for the rose garden at Farringford, to stand among the crimson and pink roses. 'The price to be the pride I shall feel in giving pleasure to the son of so great a man as Alfred Tennyson & his wife & his sons!' The grey terracotta dial is distinctive for the symbolic modelled panels, and celtic-style lettering. A motto round the dial plate (also made at Compton, though now missing) reads *'Horas non numero nisi se[renas]*. But the chief inscription quotes *In Memoriam*

For every grain of sand that runs,
And every span of shade that steals,
And every kiss of toothed wheels,
And all the courses of the suns.

when we meet,
Delight a hundredfold accrue,

Each side is devoted a member of the family, 'Alfred', 'Emily', and now that Farringford had transferred to the poet's son, 'Hallam' and 'Audrey'. The detail here, from Audrey's panel, shows an angel holding a Scandinavian symbol of the 'boat of the Sun & Moon'. 'I do like the idea of a sundial as a reminder of those who have loved a garden', Mary wrote on 11 January 1908, and of course the words were central. She instructed Hallam to find a specialist 'to orientate the dial plate on the days that are most accurate' and to cement it.

THE POET'S FURNITURE

TF 1A. THOMAS MALBY AND SON, LONDON, fl. c.1840-1900
Terrestrial globe on mahogany pedestal with mounted compass underneath, with brass fittings, 1858
41 x 29 inches, 104 x 74
Lord Tennyson, c/o Carisbrooke Castle Museum
(NETCC: 1985.5230, F69)

TF 1B. THOMAS MALBY AND SON, LONDON, fl. c.1840-1900
Celestial globe on pedestal with mounted compass underneath, 1858
41 x 29 inches, 104 x 74cm
Lord Tennyson, c/o Carisbrooke Castle Museum
(NETCC: 1985.5230, F69)

TF 2. *Mahogany pedestal writing desk, with nine drawers and black leather writing surface*
29 x 60 x 37 inches, 737 x 152.5 x 94 cm
Lord Tennyson, c/o Carisbrooke Castle Museum
(NETCC: 1985.5221, F73)

TF 3. *Carved oak armchair*
43 x 24 x 20 inches, 109.3 cm x 61 x 51 cm
Lord Tennyson, c/o Carisbrooke Castle Museum
(NETCC: 1985.5229)

TF 4. *Elm writing desk, with slope top and brass fixtures*
27 x 24 x 24 inches, 69 x 61 x 61 cm
Lord Tennyson, c/o Carisbrooke Castle Museum (NETCC: 1985.5222, F70)

TF 5. *Elm spindle-back armchair*
43 x 26 x 20 inches, 107 x 66 x 51 cm
Lord Tennyson, c/o Carisbrooke Castle Museum (NETCC: 1985.5228, C60)

TF 6. *Travelling Trunk*
Iron with foliate painted decoration
20 ½ x 32 ¾ x 17 ⅛ inches, 52 x 83 x 43.5 cm
TRC

TF 7. *Victorian Writing Table*
oak
33 ¼ x 66 ⅜ x 23 ¼ inches
84.5 x 168.5 x 59 cm
TRC

TF 8. *Victorian Writing Table*
oak, the frieze drawer stamped 'From W. Williamson & Sons, Guildford'
31x 44 x 26 ¾ inches
79 x 112 x 68 cm
TRC

TF 9: *Queen Emma's Throne*
holly and silk
50 x 24 ½ x 34 ¼ inches,
127 x 62.5 x 87 cm

Fig. 21: CAMILLE SILVY (1835-1910), *Queen Emma of Hawaii*, 16 September 1865, (National Portrait Gallery)

Queen Emma (1836-1885) widow of King Kamehameha IV of Hawaii, brought her young son and attendants to stay at Farringford on 28 September 1865. Tennyson had a throne chair made from ilex cut down from their own wood.

As the queen longed for privacy, to read letters, Emily hid her from the stream of visitors, in the summer house in the kitchen garden – 'among the cabbages', observed the queen. 'Ally and I were pleased with her sweet dignity of manner, and a calmness that made one think of an Egyptian statue'. Queen Emma's huge attendant and his wife, seated on the ground, sang and enacted Hawaiian songs and an ode to the prince, the latter in a wild monotonous chant.

The poet asked her about the vegetation of the tropics; and she invited him and Emily to stay with her to the Sandwich Islands, as Hawaii was then known. According to Tennyson's niece, Agnes Weld, he would have accepted, but for Emily's health, though he felt no vegetation could be more beautiful than an English field of buttercups: 'And we can have much of the glory of the tropics in our own gardens'. As the queen was departing on 2 October, Tennyson gave her two large magnolia blossoms from the tree growing up to the roof of Farringford.

SELECT BIBLIOGRAPHY

Mark Bills and Barbara Bryant, eds., *G. F. Watts: Victorian Visionary*, Yale University Press in association with Watts Gallery, 2008.

Jim Cheshire, ed., *Tennyson Transformed: Alfred Lord Tennyson and Visual Culture,* Farnham, Lund Humphries, 2009.

Julian Cox and Colin Ford, *Julia Margaret Cameron, The Complete Photographs* , Los Angeles, J. Paul Getty Museum, 2003.

Veronica Franklin Gould, *G. F. Watts, The Last Great Victorian* , New Haven and London, Yale University Press, 2004.

Ronald Sutherland Leveson, Lord Gower, *My Reminiscences* , London, Kegan Paul, Trench, 1883, 2 vols.

James O. Hoge, ed., *The Letters of Emily Lady Tennyson*, Pennsylvania University Press, 1974.

Elizabeth Hutchings, *Busts & Titbits: Woolner Busts & Freshwater Fragments*, Freshwater Bay, Hunnihill Publications, 2007.

Richard J. Hutchings and Brian Hinton, eds., *The Farringford Journal of Emily Tennyson 1853-1864*, Newport, Isle of Wight County Press, 1986.

Richard J. Hutchings, *Idylls of Farringford*, Freshwater Bay, Hunnihill Publications, 1965, 2006 edition.

Blanchard Jerrold, *Life of Gustave Doré*, London, W. H. Allen, 1891.

Cecil Y. Lang and Edgar F. Shannon, Jr,, eds., *The Letters of Alfred Lord Tennyson*, Oxford, 1982, 3 vols.

Robert Bernard Martin, *Tennyson, The Unquiet Heart*, Oxford, Clarendon Press, and Faber, 1980.

Vivien Noakes, ed, *Edward Lear: Selected Letters*, Oxford, Clarendon Press, 1988.

Leonée Ormond, *Alfred Tennyson: A Literary Life*, London, Macmillan 1993.

Christopher Ricks, *The Poems of Tennyson*, 1969.

Jasper Godwin Ridley, *Garibaldi*, London, Constable, 1974.

Royal Academy of Arts, London, *Edward Lear 1812-1888*, Vivien Noakes, ed, 1985.

Charles Tennyson, *Farringford: Home of Alfred Lord Tennyson*, Lincoln, Tennyson Society, 1976.

Hallam Tennyson, *Alfred Lord Tennyson: A Memoir*, London, Macmillan, 1898, 2 vols.

Ann Thwaite, *Emily Tennyson: The Poet's Wife*, London, Faber and Faber, 1996.

Mary Seton Watts, Catalogue of Watts Portraits, (ms, Watts Gallery).

 – *George Frederic Watts, The Annals of an Artist's Life*, London, Macmillan, 1912, 3 vols.

Watts Gallery, Compton, *Mary Seton Watts (1849-1938) Unsung Heroine of the Art Nouveau*, Veronica Franklin Gould, ed., 1998.

Amy Woolner, *Thomas Woolner RA, Sculptor and Poet*, London, Chapman and Hall, 1917.

INDEX

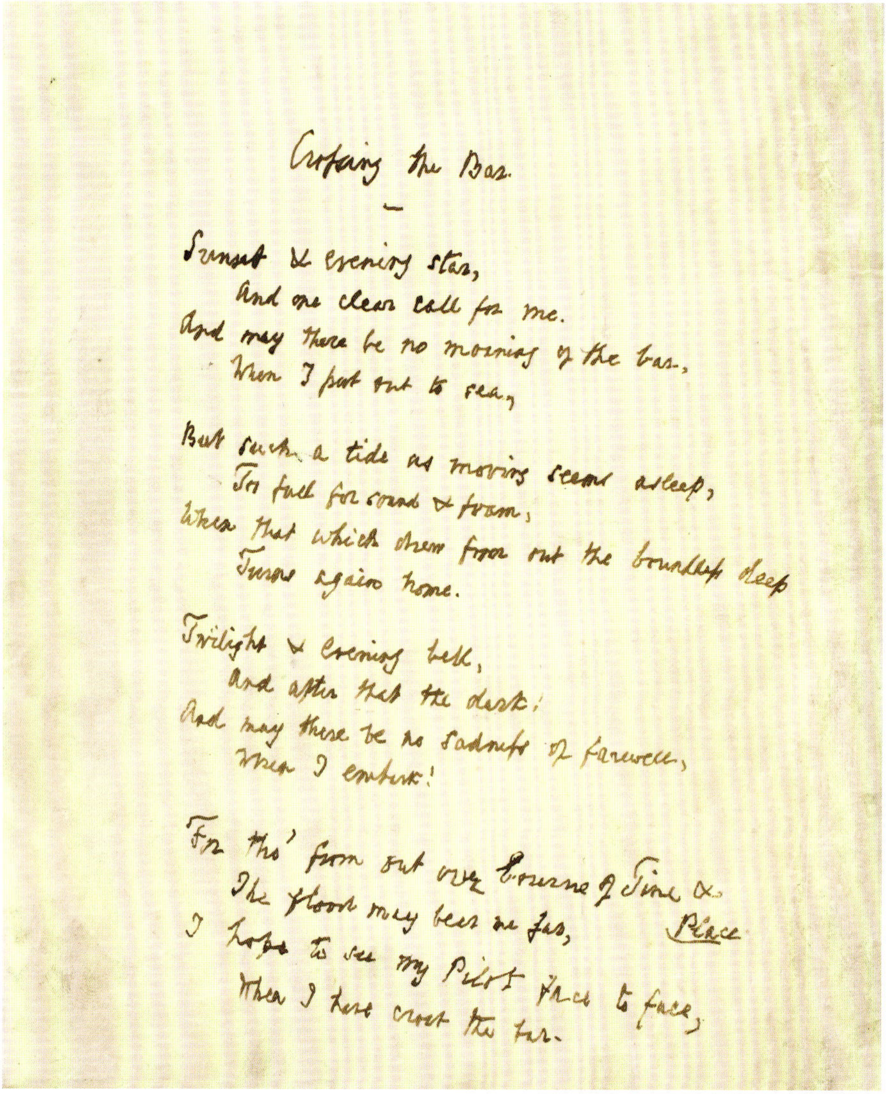

Crossing the Bar.

Sunset & evening star,
And one clear call for me.
And may there be no moaning of the bar,
When I put out to sea,

But such a tide as moving seems asleep,
Too full for sound & foam,
When that which drew from out the boundless deep
Turns again home.

Twilight & evening bell,
And after that the dark!
And may there be no sadness of farewell,
When I embark!

For tho' from out our bourne of Time & Place
The flood may bear me far,
I hope to see my Pilot face to face,
When I have crost the bar.

Fig. 22. ALFRED, LORD TENNYSON, 'Crossing the Bar'
by kind permission of Trinity College, Cambridge.